westlife
Our Story

Rob McGibbon is the author of eleven books and has written about the biggest pop groups of the last decade, from New Kids on the Block to Take That, Boyzone, Backstreet Boys and Spice Girls. He also co-wrote best-selling biographies of footballer Paul Gascoigne and Simply Red's Mick Hucknall with his father, Robin. In between writing books, Rob is a freelance journalist and writes regularly for national newspapers and magazines.

www.rob-mcgibbon.com

westlife
Our Story

Rob McGibbon

This edition first published in 2000 by
Virgin Publishing Ltd
Thames Wharf Studios
Rainville Road
London W6 9HA

First published in 1999 by Virgin Publishing Ltd

A catalogue record for the book is available from the British Library.

ISBN 0 7535 0429 4

Typeset by Phoenix Photosetting, Chatham, Kent
Printed and bound in Great Britain by
Mackays of Chatham PLC, Chatham, Kent

Contents

Author's Acknowledgements

This book has taken a considerable amount of time and work to produce. I hope you fans enjoy it and that it takes you closer to Westlife. Certainly, the book would not have been possible without the support of many people.

Firstly, I would like to thank the entire team at Virgin, especially Carolyn Thorne, Stuart Slater and James Bennett who have all worked hard pulling this project together.

My thanks also to everyone at RCA, particularly, Harry, Simon, Sonny, Tina and Sharon, for their time and enthusiasm from day one.

I am grateful to Louis Walsh for letting me write about his new boys. Without you, Louis, this would not have been possible. Cheers. My thanks also to Ronan for finding the time in a hectic schedule and to Anto for making room for one more.

My special thanks go to Shane, Kian, Mark, Nicky and Bryan, for their trust and openness in sharing their lives with me. From that bar in Brighton playing spoof, to the Stockholm Grand and the party in London, it has been a blast. I have given the book my all, more than any of my other pop books, and I hope it is something you can be proud of. You are a great bunch of guys and I wish you all the best of everything on that rollercoaster ride. Live that dream, Westlife!

Finally I would like to thank all my family for their constant love and support in everything. And here I would like to give a special mention to my mother. Thanks Ma for being such a rock to all of us kids – you're a star.

List of Illustrations

Westlife – Our Story

Budding young pop star Bryan, aged ten, plays on his synthesizer. (Westlife)
Colour studio portrait. (Andy Earl)
Bryan is the leading joker in the group. (Rob McGibbon)
The *craic* of being in Westlife. The guys laugh as they imitate the mad walk made famous by the Monkees. (Rob McGibbon)

Foreword by Ronan Keating

Hi everyone and welcome to Westlife's book. As many of you probably already know, I'm the guys' co-manager. That may sound pretty serious, but I'm not at all like a boss to them. I am their friend and advisor and I help with the artistic side of the group. I first met the guys in Dublin when Boyzone's manager Louis Walsh asked me to come along to one of the auditions for the band. I just helped out in a small way in the beginning, but I jumped at the chance when Louis asked me to be more closely involved. I could see they were a very talented bunch of guys and I was thrilled to be part of the team.

Seeing Westlife develop has been a big flashback for me. So much of what the guys are going through I have experienced with Boyzone, and there is part of me that wishes I was back there in the early days again. The guys have such an innocence and enthusiasm, and they are having so much fun. They have an amazing hunger and dedication and it has been fantastic watching them do so well. I see a bit of me in all of them and I get a shiver up my spine whenever I watch them perform. I feel very proud of them and how they have handled all the attention and pressure. I always say to them, be nice to people on the way up, then they'll be nice to you on the way down. This is what Louis taught us all in Boyzone and this is how Westlife are treating everyone, which is good to see.

The main thing for me is my friendship with the guys. I'm only a couple of years older than them, so they're like my younger brothers. When we get together we have such a laugh. I think about them all the time and worry because this business can be tough. I wouldn't be involved if I didn't like them as much as I do. They are my friends and I am always there for them. It has been an honour for me helping Westlife and I am certain the guys have a fantastic future, but the best thing is that I know they will keep their feet on the ground, no matter what happens.

This book is how the guys wanted their story told. Rob has done a great job and I know the guys love it, but, above all, I hope that you – the fans – enjoy it. This is for you. I have seen you at the shows and you've been absolutely amazing. Without your support none of this could have been possible, so on behalf of Westlife and myself, thanks a million for everything. I hope you enjoy the book and keep cheering the guys on. Take care all of you. Lots of love and God bless.

Introduction

It was just after 2 p.m. on Wednesday 14 October 1998, when I first met the boys in Westlife. A dark blue people carrier with blacked-out windows pulled up outside the Apollo Theatre in Hammersmith, west London. The side door slid open and in the back, amid the normal debris of long-distance travel, were five guys, all looking at me closely. I hardly knew anything about them, except their first names, that they were from somewhere in Ireland I'd never heard of, and that several key people in the music world thought they had the talent to make it big.

Back then, the boys were in the middle of a tour supporting Boyzone and we were on our way to Brighton for the next gig. After a quick stop to pick up a McDonald's for everyone, I set up office on the back seat to begin the first interviews that eventually led to this book. First Kian and then Shane talked about the remarkable journey which had led them to be on tour with the UK's biggest boy band. It was an astonishing story. In little more than eight months, these five guys had gone from boyhood dreams of pop stardom to singing in front of 15,000 screaming fans at world-famous arenas such as Manchester's Nynex and London's Wembley. Later, I interviewed Mark, Nicky and Bryan backstage at the Brighton Centre and then watched the group's twenty-minute set before Boyzone. The reception from the fans was incredible for what was pretty much an unknown act.

It was matched only by the precocious professionalism of the boys' set.

During the next six months, I interviewed Westlife many times in London and then in Sweden while they recorded their debut album. They all spoke to me in depth about their childhood years, their families, their ambitions, and how they rose from being everyday Irish boys to the heirs apparent of pop's boy band crown. All the interviews were punctuated by the boys' unbridled humour and easy charm and when meeting them you soon discover that they are genuine guys, who have been brought up in strong families with solid values, and know how to keep their feet on the ground. They are having the time of their lives, but they are working round the clock and treating this amazing chance with the respect it deserves.

The Westlife story began in Sligo, one of the biggest towns on the north-west coast of Ireland. It is best known as the birthplace, and resting place, of Ireland's most famous poet, William Butler Yeats. This heritage, as well as its warm, friendly people, the pretty bay and easy access to stunning countryside, has brought Sligo a healthy tourist trade. Now it is set to become more popular and famous as the birthplace of Westlife. Shane, Kian and Mark were born here and this is where the band you listen to today first started to sing. Like many youngsters, these boys grew up with wild dreams of fame and fortune, but it all seemed too fanciful to actually happen. Then, in February 1998, an amazing sequence of events brought Louis Walsh and Ronan Keating into their lives and those fantasies began to turn into reality. Soon after, Nicky and Bryan, another pair of dreamers from the Northside of Dublin, joined the group and the Westlife line up was complete. This marked the beginning of the Westlife story as most people know it. But to really understand the young men behind the latest pop sensation you have to go back to their roots in Dublin and Sligo.

Rob McGibbon

1 Shane's Story

Name:	Shane Steven Filan
Date of birth:	5 July 1979
Place of birth:	Sligo General Hospital
Star sign:	Cancer
Height:	5ft 9in/172cm
Eye colour:	Hazel/Green
Parents:	Peter and Mae
Siblings:	Finbarr, Peter, Yvonne, Liam, Denise, Mairead
Schools:	Scoil Fatima, St John's Primary, Summerhill College

Family

I come from a very close family and my mum and dad brought all us kids up to stick to one big rule: the family comes first – above everything. That understanding has kept us all really close, even as we have got older and moved away to get on with our lives.

The eldest is Finbarr. He's 30 and is an industrial engineer in the west of Ireland. Next is Peter, who is 29, and a paediatric doctor in Dublin, and then there's the first of the girls, Yvonne. She's 28 and is a teacher at Mercy College girls' school in Sligo. After her comes Liam, who is 27. He's a qualified accountant, but he gave that up to look after horses and he now runs a big horse business with my dad. After Liam there is Denise, who is 23 and works as a physiotherapist at a hospital in Dublin. Then there's Mairead, who is 21, and also lives in Dublin where she's a marketing manager. I'm the last and the baby of the bunch.

My dad, Peter, and his family have always owned restaurants, and when he moved to Sligo with my mum, Mae, in the 1960s they opened a small restaurant called The Mayfair with my uncle Luke. A little while later, when Sligo was a more happening place, they opened the Carlton Café in Castle Street, which really took off and was my family's main business for years. We were the first people in the town to make burgers and chips!

Sligo was a great place to grow up and I always love it when I get a chance to go home. My family have always lived in the house above the restaurant. It doesn't look big from the street, but it goes way back and we've built on it over the years, so it's massive now. I don't remember when all of us children were in the house together because, by the time I was six or seven, the older guys were going off to college. Our house was always full and crazy and these days it is mad at Christmas. Because so many of the family have moved away, it's a like a massive family reunion, so we have to lay on extra tables for about fifty people and it turns into an amazing party.

My mum is pretty good at organising a big party like that because she now looks after the restaurant. A good while back, my dad started buying and selling land and building up a horse business, which he now runs with Liam. They buy about twenty horses a time, look after them for six months, then sell them. Liam is amazing with horses. He can talk to them and he just clicks his fingers and they do whatever he says. That is a real talent. The horse business has gone really well and about three years ago they built a big set of stables two miles out of town. They have about fifty horses now and they also built a sanded arena, which is the biggest in our province. I wouldn't say our family is rich, but everyone works really hard and I don't think we'd be short of a few quid if it came to it.

I get on great with all of my brothers and sisters and I don't have a favourite, but Mairead and I get on especially well because our ages are so close. We used to go out to discos together and hang around in the same group of friends when we were growing up. Mairead is one of my best friends, she's great.

Because I was the youngest, I suppose I was always a bit more spoilt than the others. All my brothers looked out for me, so other kids would never dare mess with me. They'd say, 'Leave him alone, he's got big brothers,' which was great because I was always small for my my age. You wouldn't believe how small I was – I was a real midget – and everyone used to call me Shorty. We also used to have two German Shepherd dogs when I was growing up. They were called King and Kaiser. We still have Kaiser and we've got another one now called Oscar.

Sport and Horses

When I was about eight I loved watching Bruce Lee videos and got into kung fu for about a year. I was good friends with a fella called Danny in the video shop and he let me have all the films, even though I was too young. I'd watch them for hours and practise kicking like Bruce Lee around the house on cushions and just about anything that was at the right height – even my cousins and Mairead! By the time I started going to proper classes I already had a good technique and, even though I was tiny, I was better than the bigger guys. I became the King of the Spinning Kick in my club because I had the most accurate kick, but I've never really had a proper fight in my life, so I've never needed to use it seriously. I'm the type who talks my way out of a situation, but when I was younger I didn't need it anyway because I had older brothers and everyone was scared to touch me.

Horses were a major part of my family and my childhood. All of us learned to ride when we were really young. I can remember being put up in the saddle when I was only about six in the Tiny Tots class. The pony felt huge, but it was probably only small. I had a little riding hat on and all the gear and I even won a trophy. I started riding properly when I was nine, but gave it up for a few years, then went back to it. I worked with the horses every evening after school, and every weekend the whole family would go to shows all over Ireland and sometimes in England. They were massive days out for us and brilliant fun. If I ever have a family, I will encourage my children to be around horses. They are beautiful animals and if you ever get to be afraid of them, it's an awful sad thing.

I was a pretty good rider – not the best, but natural enough – and I won a lot of shows. My best moment was when I was picked to ride in the Kerry Gold Dublin Horse Show at the RDS Arena in Dublin, which is a massive showjumping event in Ireland. All my family had qualified for it over the years except me, so it was important I got in. I was twelve when I was picked, but I wasn't allowed to ride because it would have been too dangerous – I was so small and my pony was too slight. I was really upset.

We called our horses after the restaurant, so their names all started with Carlton. We had a grey called Carlton Guy for about fifteen years. He was like the family's pet pony and all of us learned to ride on him for about the first four years. His nickname was Jasper and if I could find him now I would buy him back. He would be about 23 now and the last I heard he was in Scotland, but he may even be dead. He was a brilliant pony. One of my other favourites was Carlton Flight. He was the last pony I had and I nicknamed him Condor. He was a gorgeous-looking brown pony, with wonderful features, and we still have him. Michael Keirns is the jockey who rides him now. He's a genius and has won Best Jockey on him two years in a row at Under 14s and 15s. We bought Condor for only £500, but he is so good now he is worth a fortune. At one point I was going to follow Liam and work with horses full time when I left school, but I went to college instead and then the band came up and everything took off.

I used to like Gaelic football and soccer at school. When I was twelve, I played in goal while Liam took shots. He wasn't shooting hard, so I said, 'Hit it properly, will ya,' and then he really whacked it and I broke my wrist trying to stop the ball.

The only sport I felt passionate about – apart from horses – was rugby. I played at fly half and was in the Connaught team. When I was eighteen, I started taking it very seriously and had trials for the Irish team. I did well and got to the third stage, but then the band started getting more serious. I had to work out whether I wanted to make it in rugby, or try to make platinum records and sing for big crowds. During the trials, me and the guys were preparing for a show and I realised I might get injured and not be able to sing. The thought of that scared the hell out of me and I suddenly lost interest in rugby and forgot about it. If you are serious about anything, you've got to be totally committed. I realised that all I wanted was to hear my songs on the radio and that was when singing became my life.

Music

I have loved singing ever since I can remember. The first song I really got into was 'Uptown Girl' by Billy Joel, which my mum bought for me on tape. It was the first I ever owned and I played it all the time. I also loved 'All Night Long' by Lionel Richie. I was only four when those songs came out, but I knew all the words and was always singing along to them and watching the videos on *Top of the Pops*. Although I had a good voice, I was really shy and was afraid to get up and sing in front of people when I was young. My mum was always so proud of her kids and she used to encourage me to sing. Fair plays to her because she gave me and all us kids confidence in ourselves. Thanks Mum for that. Whenever we had relatives over, all us kids would have to get up and do our bit. Mairead was a champion at Irish dancing, so she would have to get up and dance. Peter was a great boxer and was once ranked number four in Ireland, so he would show off his trophies. We all had to do something and I would get up and sing for everyone.

My whole world changed when Michael Jackson brought out the *Bad* album when I was about eight or nine. He took over my life and from then on I wanted to *be* Michael Jackson. I watched his videos for hours and learned how to dance like him. I would push back the chairs in the room and learn his dance moves. I even taught myself to moonwalk. I had all the videos he ever made, every single and album. I was the biggest Michael Jackson fan in Sligo and I even had a shiny glove and hats like him. I would ring up the record shop to find out when his latest song was coming out, so I would be the first to get it in the town. All I dreamed of was being on stage and having screaming fans just like him. Even when I was at school I would daydream about being Michael Jackson, the most famous pop star in the world. I loved his music above everything for years, especially songs like 'The Way You Make Me Feel' and 'Man In The Mirror'. For years I wanted to see him in concert and then I managed to get a ticket for his History tour in July 1997. I was in the middle of the crowd only about 100 yards from him. He was amazing and, to me, it was like watching Elvis. I thought Michael Jackson was a god. His music has changed a lot since he started, but I still think he is a brilliant artist.

The first proper stage show I was in was *Grease* at the Hawkswell Theatre in Sligo when I was twelve. All the main parts were for adults or much older kids, so I nearly didn't bother auditioning. I was also really afraid and didn't believe I could sing that well. When you're little you think millions of people are better than you and that everyone will laugh at you. My brother Finbarr gave me a hard time about being afraid and he said, 'You've got a great voice, don't hide it all your life, do something about it.' I'm glad he was like that because it stirred me up and I went for the audition. There wasn't really a role for someone as young as me, but the producer created a special part for me and a girl called Olwyn Morgan to sing a duet called 'We Go Together'.

I couldn't believe the reaction we got – it was amazing. I was only tiny and the stage seemed so huge. There were about 350 people in the audience and for a few minutes they were all looking at me and this girl. I have got that show on video and it's so funny. I have got such a little voice and it was so high – I could sing some serious high notes back then – and I loved to dance. For a few minutes I thought I was Michael Jackson and I loved it. I came out for the encore and was dancing away. Everyone was clapping and it was like they were cheering for me. I felt so happy and it was at that moment I realised

I wanted to be a performer. I'll never forget after the show when my mum came over and picked me up and gave me a big hug. She was so proud. I felt so sad when that run of *Grease* was over, but it gave me confidence and after that I started to love the theatre.

When I was fourteen I went to my secondary school, Summerhill College, which was an all-boys school. Summerhill teamed up with the Ursuline College girls' school every year to do musicals, and that's when I got into singing and acting in a big way. I did *Annie Get Your Gun*, but had to play a girl. I was dressed up in a skirt and a bonnet, but there were other lads dressed as girls so we could see the funny side. After that, people started to recognise me as a singer and I got lead roles and I started doing shows at the Hawkswell regularly as well. I was the Artful Dodger in *Oliver* at school and in a production at the theatre. I preferred singing to acting, but doing shows was the hobby I loved above everything. I used to worry about my height when I was a teenager, but I realised that when you're on stage it doesn't matter at all.

It is amazing what a big part the show *Grease* has played in my life. We did it at school when I was fifteen and I played Kenickie and Kian was Sonny. A couple of years later we did *Grease* again and I was Danny and Kian was Kenickie. I got to know Kian through the shows. He only lived about a mile from my house but we never really hung out together because I was a year ahead of him in school. We just did the shows and went off with our own group of friends. I also got to know Mark through the musicals.

I was a big Boyzone fan at school, but I always got laughed at because it wasn't really cool to like them back then. I was knocked out by their style and success and I couldn't believe a bunch of Irish lads could do that. It really made me want to be in a pop group. The very first idea I had was with my friend Michael Garrett – we thought of starting a four piece and calling it SC4, after Summerhill College. Everyone was laughing at us for wanting to do that. I asked Kian if he was interested and he just laughed as well. He was really into heavy rock music back then and he just said, 'A boy band? You've got to be joking!'

Michael and I got another two lads interested and fixed up to have a rehearsal, but they didn't show up and that was the end of it. It was all talk at this stage and it never led to anything. To be honest, I didn't really think anything would ever happen. I thought you had to be someone important in Dublin to stand a chance of getting into a pop group, not just a normal lad from Sligo.

Girls

The first girl I kissed was Fran Keirans. She was a wee blonde girl and I'll never forget it. I was only seven, but our two families used to go to the horse shows together all the time. Fran was my first girlfriend and we used to hold hands, put our arms around each other and stuff like that. There we were in our little jodhpurs, it was mad and just a kiddies' thing. I'm still friends with Fran and her family. My next girlfriend was Orla Kilroy and I had my first proper kiss with her. I was only ten at the time. I met Orla through Irish dancing. My sister Mairead wasn't really into horseriding, but she was a brilliant dancer and she won the All Ireland Championships and came 24th in the world one year. She won just about all there is to win at Irish dancing and I would go to the dancing competitions to watch.

My mum would say to me, 'You don't want to go to the dancing, Shane, go horseriding, you'll have more

Shane enjoys an ice cream.

fun.' And I would say, 'Oh no, it's OK, Mum, I don't mind.' The reason I wanted to go was because I met loads of girls at the shows. I would go with a couple of mates and all the girls would look gorgeous with their hair done up. We'd act like cool little men and be disappearing round the back with the girls, but not in a bad way. I liked being around girls when I was younger and I always liked to have a girlfriend, but I didn't have mad serious relationships. The girls used to think I was a funny little fella and they would ask Mairead, 'Where's your brother?' Those Irish dancing shows were great fun.

When I was about fifteen, I went out with a girl who was in *Grease* when I was Kenickie. We went out together for just over a year, but broke up three times in total. She broke it off for a day, then we got back together, and then I broke it off for a few days. The two of us broke it off the third time because it was just not working out. I had bought her a Valentine's card around that time, but I never sent it. I still see her around Sligo and we get on well. My head was wrecked after we broke up and I waited for a couple of months before I went out with anyone else. Then I started really enjoying myself. I had been tied down for a year which was stupid at such a young age. I enjoyed being in a relationship, but, to be honest, I think it was a bit too young to be so serious. After that I went out with girls for just a few months here and there.

Everything has become harder for us with relationships since we've been in the band. It is difficult to keep in touch, especially when we are touring, but it is still possible to go out with girls, especially at home.

2 Kian's Story

Name:	Kian John Francis Egan
Date of birth:	29 April 1980
Place of birth:	Sligo General Hospital
Star sign:	Taurus
Height:	5ft 10in/175cm
Eye colour:	Blue
Parents:	Kevin and Patricia
Siblings:	Viv, Gavin, Fenella, Tom, Marielle, Colm
Schools:	Scoil Ursla, St John's Primary, Summerhill College

Family

Like Shane, I'm also from a big family. We have always lived in the same house, about a ten-minute walk out of Sligo, and I had a wonderful childhood there. I have a great relationship with both my parents and all my brothers and sisters – we all love each other very much. My dad, Kevin, is an electrician who works for the ESB (Irish electricity board) and my mum, Patricia, has been a full-time mum and housewife. With seven of us, she's been kept pretty busy. My mum says to me, 'If you make it, Kian, I would like to open a kids' clothes shop.'

If everything goes well with the band, I'd love to help her do that.

My dad always made sure us kids got anything we needed. He has always been devoted to the family and helping us get on in life. Whatever we wanted to do, he helped us out and you can't ask for more than that. Both my parents are brilliant and if it wasn't for them I wouldn't be here doing this with the band. They always supported me in everything and gave me confidence in myself. My parents encouraged all of us to try anything we wanted and we were always kept busy. Just trying things made us confident people and I love my parents for being like that. I'm very lucky to have them.

The youngest in the family is Colm, who is only four, so he doesn't really do much. Then there is Marielle, who is thirteen and is in secondary school. She grew up listening to Boyzone and is mad into the pop scene, so she thinks it's cool that I'm in a band. She listens to our songs and loves them. Marielle is very musical, too, and plays the violin and piano and has been in a girl band herself, but only in a small way.

It's me after Marielle and then Tom, who is 22. He is studying architecture at college and is also the bass player in a rock band called Fiction. After Tom comes Fenella, who is 24. She is a legal secretary and has two children. Then there is Gavin, who is 28 and is a secondary school teacher and a music lecturer at Sheffield University. Finally there is Viv, who is 30, and she works as a town planner in Roscommon. I am really close to all my brothers and sisters, but I suppose Fenella is my closest sister and Tom would be my closest brother simply because we were the same age group when we were growing up. If I have a problem now, with girlfriends or something to do with the band, I would talk to Tom and Fenella.

I shared a room with Tom when I was a kid and we used to fight like mad and kill each other, like all brothers do. He was a lot stronger than me, but I would hit him hard in the right places and get away with it because I was younger. Despite all the fighting, though, we were like best mates and went to parties together when we were older. He was always very supportive because he had been through things I was going through just a few years earlier. He gave me lots of advice, about school and relationships, and he looked out for me like all big brothers. He is also into music and is very proud of what we are doing. I also have a cousin called Gillian, who is like another sister to me. We grew up together and hung around in the same crowd of friends. She has been like an extra presence in my life and a big support.

Music and Sport

When I was four, I went in for my first talent competition, which is called a *feis* (pronounced 'fesh') in Ireland. They're a big tradition in our country and it's where kids get to perform anything they want: poetry reading, singing, dancing, playing an instrument; you can do just about anything. At my first one I recited a poem called 'Whispers' at a hotel in Sligo. I won and I still have the little trophy. I was never really nervous, even in the beginning, because my mum had built all this confidence into me. As far as she was concerned there was nothing I couldn't do, so I was eager to have a go. It all started there and I went on to do music, acting, dancing and then bands.

All my family are musical and I started playing piano

when I was nine. My eldest brother Gavin was a part-time piano teacher and we had a piano in the house, so he gave me lessons and took me all the way up to grade four. I was not 100 per cent into piano because it was all classical music, which I thought was pretty boring, so I didn't take it much higher. I was really into rock bands, so I started playing guitar and actually taught myself before I had any proper lessons. By the time I was fourteen, I could play tunes by ear if I heard them on the radio, and then I started learning chords and got involved in rock bands. Gavin played lead guitar in a pub band called The Lemon Aftermats and I used to watch him and his mates rehearsing in the garage and have a go on the drums and stuff. My mum would be on at me to practise my piano, but I didn't like it too much because I wanted to play loud instruments like electric guitar. I was surrounded by music throughout my childhood and I can play ten or twelve instruments. I'm not brilliant at them all, but I could pick up an instrument and play a tune on it.

Our house was always full of music. My sisters played violins, one brother played trombone, someone was always on the piano, and there was me on the guitar – there were all these noises coming from different rooms. If I wasn't playing music, I was always busy doing something else and never had a spare night when I was growing up. During the week, after school, I would have jazz and tap dancing lessons, clarinet lessons, piano classes, guitar, hurling or basketball, then football training and drama classes. At the weekends I played football matches and crammed in anything else I could. I was never sitting around doing nothing. My parents encouraged me in every direction they could, but they were always saying, 'Kian, you've got to study, get your studies done and then you can do anything you want.'

Girls

I got married for the first time when I was seven! The wedding was at the back of an empty old house in the street where I lived. All us boys used to do it because it was a way of getting to kiss a girl. My first 'wife' dressed up in a white communion dress and I put on my bow tie. It was a big serious thing for us in the street – I even had a best man. I think that marriage only lasted a few days, then I got a divorce and married someone else. It was a great laugh and it gave us a good excuse to snog a different girl. It was mad, but great fun.

When I was younger, I used to hang around in a big crowd of girls and guys and we always had a great time. The only problem for me was the hassle I got from some troublemakers. There was a rough bunch of lads who would be drinking in the street and looking for fights, and when I was about thirteen or fourteen I was a marked boy. I don't know why but they always picked on me and I often ended up worse off because they were bigger and older than me. One guy in particular was always after me. He was the big bad bully, and it would stop me going out to certain discos because I was afraid of running into him. He was always looking for trouble. I would be doing absolutely nothing and he would come up and hit me. It was crazy and it upset me, but one time he hit me and I fought back. It was just a natural reaction and I turned round and crocked him. He got hurt and he left me alone after that. I saw him in a nightclub in Sligo not so long ago; this was when things were going well with the band. He wanted to talk to me and be pals. No way was I interested – I won't forget how he treated me.

I fell seriously in love when I met Sonya when I was fifteen. She was my first true love and I went out with her for a year and a half. It was very serious and we spent pretty much every day together. After about four months together I told her that I loved her. It wasn't just saying it like kids do – we *were* in love. I would meet her after school and walk her home, then see her later in the night after we'd done our homework. We would go to the cinema together, down to the beach, or to the waterfalls, or just stay in and watch TV together. We went everywhere together and it was very romantic. It was brilliant and idyllic because we were so in love. We were as serious as couples are when they're in their twenties. Even now I can't believe how serious it was. I'm telling you, we were crazy for each other.

A lot of our friends were in couples at that time, so we had such a laugh together. We were quite mature for fifteen-year-olds and we went to pubs and discos. We looked a lot older than our age and we had fake IDs just in case we got any problems. We had such a good time, but Sonya and I were just as happy lying around cuddling and watching TV together.

We broke up three times because of exams, but we always got back together. Then one day she asked me to come round to her house and I thought, grand, but when I saw her, she said, 'I want to break up with you.' I couldn't believe it and I was saying, 'What . . . why . . . we can't!' Sonya broke my heart to pieces on the spot. I begged her to think about it, but she never called me after that day. It was just, BOOM, see ya! I would see her around town in the pubs or the discos and I would start crying. Just seeing her would ruin my night and I would get my mates to talk to her and get her to change her mind, but she wouldn't which only made things worse.

It took me six months to get over Sonya and I was so upset I cried in bed every night. We had a brilliant year and a half together and I will always have a place in my heart for her. I saw her in a disco in Sligo a while back and I told her I still loved her and she said, 'Oh shut up Kian, you're drunk.' She was right. Our relationship was a long time ago, but it's good that we can be friends and laugh about the old times.

A girl called Yvonne was my second love. I started going out with her about a year after I broke up from Sonya. That was also pretty serious, but we kept breaking up over stupid things. I broke up with her three times because I didn't really want to have another serious relationship. I kept thinking, I have to get out of this, but then I would want to get back with her. We were together for eleven months, but then she broke up with me which was pretty upsetting. Looking back now, though, I know it was for the best, and I'm still friends with her.

The last relationship I had lasted about three months. I was going out with her during the Boyzone tour in 1998. It was going really well, but I was away for three weeks solid while we were on tour and when I came back to Ireland it was obvious it wasn't working out, so we agreed to break up. Since I've been in the band, a lot of people have got me down as the Romeo of the group, which upsets me a bit because that really isn't me. I get on well with girls, but I'm definitely not a womaniser or anything like that. When it comes to relationships, I'm a hopeless romantic and I'm looking forward to the day I fall in love again and find that special girl.

Musicals

From when I was about ten, I dreamed of being a rock star. I used to love bands like Metallica, Guns N'Roses, Iron Maiden and Bon Jovi, and I was always practising loud guitar solos and jamming with friends. Four of us formed a band which lasted for a long while. Our first name was Scrod, but we went through various names. We were called Pyromania for a while and then we became Hallucination. That was our last name before we split up.

Being in that band was great fun. We were trying to be hard and write songs, but we mainly did cover versions of our favourite rock songs. 'Wild Thing' was the very first song we played and we used to rehearse after school and at weekends. We had long hair and did crazy guitar solos and generally took the mickey out of it all. We wanted to be the next Metallica and we played a few gigs around Sligo. One time we went into a talent contest and won £500. We had really good instruments and we could make an amazing noise, so we weren't bad. My dad was really good to me and made sure I got any instrument I wanted, and when I was fifteen he bought me a guitar that cost £400, so you can see we were pretty serious. I was really into the rock thing. It's amazing to think of that now!

I started doing musicals at the Hawkswell Theatre and at school. I was only a background dancer at first, but then I got better parts and that's when I really started to like the idea of being on stage. I did shows like *The Pajama Game*, *West Side Story*, *Annie Get Your Gun* and *Oliver!* and various pantomimes. I used to love it and was probably in about twenty productions in all.

Grease was the big show for me and that's where Shane and I really got to know each other. I had known him on and off all my life, but we were never great mates who hung around together. When we started doing musicals, we got on well and I thought he was very talented and had a great voice.

He didn't think much of the rock stuff I was doing and I remember thinking it was daft to try and do a boy band. The big turning point came for me when I saw what Take

**Kian laughs during dinner at TGI Friday
in Stockholm.**

That were doing when they were at their peak. I loved
songs like 'Everything Changes' and 'Pray' and used to
watch their videos and dream about being on stage like
them. It really opened up my mind. Then Boyzone
happened, and then the Backstreet Boys came along and I
loved their style. They looked cool and their songs were
brilliant and that's when I thought, A boy band? Yeah,
that's for me.

3 Mark's Story

Name:	Mark Michael Patrick Feehily
Date of birth:	28 May 1981
Place of birth:	Sligo General Hospital
Star sign:	Gemini
Height:	5ft 10½in/176cm
Eye colour:	Blue
Parents:	Oliver and Marie
Siblings:	Barry and Colin
Schools:	Calry National,
	St Patrick's Primary,
	Summerhill College

Family

My mum, Marie, is a civil servant and works in the department of agriculture. She is originally from Sligo and has lived there for most of her life, and her family owned a pub in the town. My dad, Oliver, was brought up on a farm in an area just outside Sligo, and that's where I was brought up and still live. He owns a window company now and is very good at working with his hands.

I am the eldest boy in my family, then there is Barry, who is fourteen. He's even more shy than me and is really into horses and is mad about cars. You just have to give him a name of a car and he'll tell you all about it – the speed it goes, the size of the engine, how much it costs, he knows the whole lot. Then there is Colin, who is nine. He's soccer mental and a crazy Manchester United fan. He goes to every game for the local team, Sligo Rovers, and always drags my dad and grandfather along. Anything to do with football and Colin loves it.

My brothers aren't mad interested in the band. They are too young to read newspapers and don't really know what is going on. It hasn't really affected them, but they ask me to get autographs if I meet any famous people. I am close to Barry and Colin, but we are not the sort of brothers who hug each other all the time and spend hours sitting down chatting. I'm more likely to get them in headlocks and stuff like that.

When I was a baby I had trouble sleeping, so my mum used to put the radio on when she left me in the cot in her bedroom. The noise relaxed me and helped me get to sleep, and I always had the radio on at night for years after that. These days I still can't go to sleep without a radio or a television on. It doesn't matter what is on – it could be MTV or an old black and white film – just as long as there is noise in the room. It might seem a bit weird, but that's how I sleep. When I am travelling with the band, I get the room on my own, because I need the TV on to get to sleep, which keeps the others awake. When we were on the Boyzone tour, I was first sharing with Bryan and then Shane and they both had trouble sleeping with the television on, but without the noise I didn't have a hope in hell. It's easier for me to have the single room, and now I've bought a portable CD player, so I also play music to get me to sleep.

Growing up and School

My home is in a small area just outside Sligo. It is only two and a half miles from the centre of town, but that's like being in the country. My house is surrounded by loads of beautiful fields and is quite secluded, but in recent years there has been so much building that the town is growing out to us. I suppose we'll end up being part of Sligo eventually.

My first school was a small local infants, and then I went to St Patrick's National, which was also quite a small school with only about 300 kids. It was about four miles out of town, so it was very quiet and friendly. I enjoyed it there, although I was totally off the point in class. I was a total daydreamer and I made one teacher's life hell because my mind was never on studying. I was always talking, or distracting other kids, or looking out the window and singing to myself. I didn't mean to be badly behaved, and I was not a troublemaker, but it's just that my mind was elsewhere.

I used to play a lot of tennis at school. I was dead serious about my tennis and would play every single day and travel round Ireland playing for Connaught province. There are four provinces in Ireland and at the end of the year there was a big round robin tennis competition. I played twice for Connaught at Under 12s and Under 14s and did pretty well, but never won the whole thing.

I loved tennis so much and for a while I wanted to be a professional player, but I realised that wasn't really going to be possible. We just didn't have the facilities or the coaching in my area to take you to a higher level. Unless you were willing to pay a lot of money and travel to Dublin every weekend for proper coaching, you didn't stand a chance. Tennis is great fun, so I just enjoyed playing and stopped taking it so seriously. I also got into playing squash and badminton a lot as well.

When I was twelve, I left my local school and went to Summerhill College in Sligo, which was a massive change for me. I had to travel into town every day and there were like a thousand boys in that school. Up until then I would only have gone to town with my mum on Saturdays, or very occasionally with friends, so you could say I was not as mature or as 'with it' as the other lads. The kids from the town were used to hanging around the shops in gangs or going to lively places on a daily basis, but I had never done all that before. I was used to staying at home, or going to watch television at a friend's house over the road, or going to my gran's house in the evenings. My social life was just staying at home and playing with my cousins, which was very boring to the Sligo guys. So it was quite a shock for me to go to Summerhill, and I was very wary of everything at first. I was very reserved and shy during my first two years because I was worried the other boys would see me as a farmer's kid, so I stuck with the friends I knew from my last school. I'm a shy person, so it took me a while to settle in at Summerhill.

Acting and Singing

For as long as I can remember I have loved singing. I used to jump up and down on my bed with a hairbrush in my hand pretending it was a microphone, thinking I was a pop star. The first song I can remember really liking was 'Uptown Girl' by Billy Joel. I used to sing that during playtime at my first school when I was about four.

Every Sunday evening, all my family would go to my grandparents' house and the main event was when everyone had to get up and do a party piece. I knew I could sing OK, so I usually did a song. I enjoyed it so much, even though I was so shy, and that's when I realised I liked performing. I would normally be all shy in front of a load of people, but I didn't have nerves or anything when I was singing. Those party pieces were a big influence on me, but the only problem I had was remembering the words. I was really bad at that and would end up humming a lot of the time! I started entering talent competitions when I was about seven. They were only small things in my local area, but I loved them and won a plaque one year for singing. When I was in the second year at my junior school, I came first in a talent competition and won a trophy and £50, which was amazing money to me.

I also used to sing in the school choir, but the biggest influence on me when I was younger was going to see musicals at the local theatre. It used to send shivers up my spine and make the hairs on the back of my neck stand up. I would sit there wishing I could be on the stage like the other kids, but I always thought you had to be someone special and really talented to get a chance. I didn't have any idea how you went about getting into musicals, but then one year, when I was about nine, my cousin Gail, who is a couple of years younger than me, was in a pantomime. She sang 'Yellow Bird' on stage and I remember watching her, thinking, Maybe I can get up and do that too.

When I was about ten, I did my first show, which was *Scrooged*. Then I got a part in *West Side Story*, which was the first show I did at the Hawkswell Theatre. It was a production for adults, but there were four parts for kids and I played an American boy. I was only on stage for five minutes, but I was really nervous on the first night. The show ran for three weeks and was so popular it was booked out for the whole time. We won an amateur theatre award and it was just about the most exciting thing that had ever happened to me. I remember my parents being really proud of me. They have always supported me, no matter what I wanted to do.

The other big influence on my life was seeing the movie *Grease* when my dad got us our first video recorder. My mum's cousin lent us about twenty or thirty tapes and I came across *Grease* in that collection. When I first watched it, I couldn't believe that such a brilliant film existed. It had a big effect on me and I watched it again and again. I'm not joking, I watched that film every single minute of the day when I was off school. I used to put on my father's old leather jacket and pretend I was Danny. The jacket was nothing like a biker's jacket, but I wasn't bothered. I used to stand in front of the mirror singing the songs – I knew all the words.

There is something about *Grease* – it's weird how it kept coming back and playing a part in my life. I know it has had a big impact on Shane and Kian too. The first time I saw it as a stage show was at the Hawkswell Theatre when I was about ten or eleven. Shane was in it and he came on and sang 'We Go Together' with a girl from Sligo. I didn't know Shane at all back then. I was in the audience with my mum thinking he was good and had a great voice. Watching him really hit me and made me even more determined to get into musicals. I loved the whole vibe about the theatre and was desperate to be involved. It's amazing that watching Shane had such an influence on me, especially when you think how everything has turned out with the band.

Summerhill College put on a big show every year and the first I did was *Annie Get Your Gun* and then *Oliver!*, but I was only in the chorus in these. Shane played the Artful Dodger in *Oliver!*. When I was in the third year the school put on *Grease* and that was the first time I really got to sing properly in a show. Shane was Kenickie and Kian was Sonny in that production and I got to know them pretty well while we were rehearsing together after school.

I admired Shane for being a deadly singer and I liked the other lads. I remember just before a show one night, Shane and Kian and some guys were trying to push people in the showers at the gym and finally they got me. It was just for a laugh, but I was in the wrong place at the wrong time. I was fully clothed and had to go home to change, which was a disaster, but I got back in time and the show still went brilliantly. I was Johnny Casino and Teen Angel and had three solos. That was the first time I actually let myself go and sang on stage with a mike and an audience in front of me. Singing the Hand Jive with the whole cast – but with me as the main singer – was a major moment for me. The only bad thing was the top I was wearing, which had a glittery American flag on it and looked tragic. But I felt amazing and that is when I really got into being a singer. All of a sudden I was doing what I wanted to do – it was just a brilliant feeling. For the first two years of school, I had so much wanted to be involved in the main line-up and now I was there and it felt incredible. That show changed everything for me and was a big turning point in my life. I had always had the feeling deep inside that I wanted to be a singer, but this really reinforced it in my mind and I loved it. It made me realise that I wanted to be a professional actor or singer.

Around this time, I had a job in a sports shop because I wanted to earn some money and be more independent. A production of *Oliver!* was being cast at the Hawkswell. A friend of mine was in the show, but I was too busy with the job to get involved. He kept asking me to come down and audition and I was in a such a dilemma. I couldn't do the show and the job at the same time, so I had to make a choice. Finally, I decided to throw in the job and do the show. That was a big decision for me, but one of the best I've ever made. That's when I made a deliberate choice to make the musicals my priority and I'm so pleased I did. After that, my life revolved around plays and musicals.

Most of the main parts in that *Oliver!* show had gone by the time I auditioned, but I played a barman and a bookseller and it was great. It was a very professional show and I loved all the rehearsals. I had such a brilliant laugh with everyone and that was probably my favourite musical because so much preparation went into it. And it was because of that show that I got parts in other productions. The crowd of people who were involved in *Oliver!* went on to do all the other shows together and that's how I got to know Shane and Kian so well. I was in *Godspell* and *The Pajama Game* and did about three or four shows a year at the Hawkswell and school after that. I would always get a local paper in Sligo called *The Weekender*, which had a column called Bits and Pieces, and look for all the details of auditions and shows coming up. I was really buzzing and getting confidence and I lived for doing a show. I would hate it when they ended.

I did a few other part-time jobs when I was a teenager. I worked in a restaurant where they always played 'Words' by Boyzone, which was in the charts at the time. That is my least favourite Boyzone song because it always reminds me of cleaning toilets and working there. I also worked in Burger King, which was my worst job. It was a new restaurant and it took us ages to learn how to clean everything at the end of each day, so we were kept working until 5am on a Friday night. It ruined my weekends and I couldn't cope with the lack of sleep, so I chucked that job in.

Mark prepares for a photo shoot.

I am at my happiest when I am singing – I love it. I feel really comfortable when I'm on stage. A lot of my inhibitions go and I am not the same person as I am off stage. I am not quiet anymore, I let myself go. I feel totally different.

Girls

I used to have girlfriends every now and then, but nothing very serious. I never really had them for a long time, and the longest relationship I've had was about three months or something like that. My first crush was on a girl in primary school, whose mother worked with my mum. I would walk her home from school. She was never actually my girlfriend or anything like that. She was a couple of years older than me and I would send Valentine's cards to her without signing them. It was a puppy love kind of thing. My first kiss was when I was thirteen; it was with a girl from Sligo at my neighbour's house during a party for the French student exchange trip.

Getting serious just hasn't been for me yet. When I started going out more as I got older, I liked to meet different girls and not be tied down. I've never really had a problem meeting girls because I have always looked older than my age. When I was sixteen, I looked eighteen, so I could get into clubs. I went to Equinox in Sligo a few times with Shane, but I never really bothered going to pubs. There has never really been one special girl for me. Even the girl I went out with for three months was not serious. I have just never got involved and I suppose it will be even harder for me now that the band has taken off. At the moment, I wouldn't like to have a serious relationship or commitment. I'm too young and there's loads of time for all that. Now people are starting to know who we are, I might be a bit more cautious when I'm meeting girls; I'll try to make sure they are genuine before I get involved.

4 Talented T-Birds

During the late summer of 1996, Mary McDonagh, the producer at the Hawkswell Theatre, announced that one of the shows in the forthcoming autumn season would be *Grease*. Shane, then seventeen and in his final year at school, had grown into the leading star in Sligo and was the natural choice for Danny, the love-struck teenager from Rydell High. Kian would be his wise-cracking sidekick Kenickie, and Mark would play Vince Fontaine and Teen Angel. The T-Birds, the leather-jacketed group of lads who idolise Danny, were to be played by other budding young performers from Summerhill College, including Shane's friend Michael Garrett, another close pal, Derek Lacey, and an older boy called Graham Keighron, who was not in school. It was a strong cast and rehearsals in the evenings after school soon showed that this looked like being a special production. Certainly Shane, Kian and Mark had grown into their roles, thanks to their previous *Grease* performances, and now they were older, their voices were stronger and their acting was more confident.

A considerable buzz about the show went round Sligo as the October opening drew closer. And the first night audience were not disappointed. The show was a smash hit and the most slick and exciting production the town had seen for years.

Grease instantly became the hottest ticket in Sligo, but there was one major problem – it was only on for five nights and the clamour for tickets far outstripped supply. As the run continued, the Hawkswell's box office was besieged with ticket requests, and Mary McDonagh was left in no doubt that she had a hit show on her hands, albeit on a small scale. There were demands for the show to be kept running until everyone got to see it, but that was impossible because the theatre was already booked for the next two months. In this case, it appeared the show could not go on.

As the curtain came down on the last night, Shane, Kian and Mark, and the rest of the cast, slipped out of their costumes, washed away the make-up and adjourned to the foyer bar for a celebratory drink. Everyone associated with the show was on a high as they shared the *craic*, the Irish term for general chat and banter.

It was during this after-show party that the very first line of the incredible Westlife story began. As the initial excitement of the party cooled into a more mellow mood, Shane and Mark started humming a song. They were always singing something together, so this was nothing unusual. The song was 'I'll Make Love To You', a moving *a cappella* love song which had been a number five hit two years earlier for Boyz II Men, one of the guys' favourite bands. Gradually, the other lads in the T-Bird gang joined in until all six boys were singing in perfect harmony. Silence spread throughout the rest of the party as everyone listened to the sweet sound. When the song ended, there were some cheers and applause from around the foyer and one girl said enthusiastically, 'Wow, that was brilliant. You guys should do something with that.' It was a nice compliment, but was lost in the merriment of the night as the singing and joking continued. That girl's enthusiasm, however, did help sow the seed of an idea.

Grease was such a success that Mary McDonagh had to bow to public demand and reschedule the show at the earliest opportunity. She decided it would return for a run of four nights in December. It was during this time, before the show's second run, that the six boys plotted to do – just as that girl had suggested – *something* with their undoubted singing skills. They decided to form a group and perform what they thought would be a one-off gig, something that would a be a lot of fun, but nothing too serious.

They began rehearsing some songs and gathered at various houses to watch Take That, Boyzone and Backstreet Boys videos for hours on end. They analysed the dance moves and watched the real pop stars, closely looking for clues to the magic of their success. Gradually the boys built up a thirty-minute set of cover versions and arranged to play their first gig. They had flyers made and put an ad in the local newspaper that announced the arrival of 'Sligo's very own Boyzone'.

The news spread rapidly through Summerhill College, as well as other schools and the town, and the interest escalated. The venue was the function room at the Southern Hotel, where the boys were the headline act during a fashion show for teenagers. It was a modest start, with about 300 young girls watching, but on a local level this was tantamount to Wembley Arena for the guys.

Kian remembers that night fondly: 'It is amazing to think back to that show now. That was the real beginning of the band. After *Grease*, we were really up for having a go and worked hard at getting a proper act together. The moment we came out on stage and started singing 'I'll Never Break Your Heart', the place went crazy. Girls were screaming like mad. It was like nothing we had ever experienced. Shane and Mark sang the leads, but the whole band gelled perfectly from the word go. We dressed up in different-coloured tops and the noise was amazing. Nothing like that had been done in Sligo before and it went down a smash. We had planned the show ourselves and knew what we were trying to do, so when it all went down well it meant a lot. After the show we were mobbed by the girls and that's when we all realised that this was something worth sticking with.'

Shane adds: 'That night at the Southern Hotel was when I got my first buzz off being in a boy band, and from then on I wanted to be in a pop group. Before that, I wanted to be in shows and be an actor. But this was so exciting and it was like, YES, this is what we want to do. We had done the gig just for the *craic* and never really took it seriously, but the reception we got was incredible. After the show it was mad. Loads of people were coming up asking for our autographs and asking us to sing things for them. All us guys were thinking, This is great, we love this. We felt like we were in Boyzone for a night. It was amazing. We always loved singing, but we never thought we could really do anything serious with it, but that got us thinking.'

The six boys were so knocked out by the success at the Southern Hotel that they could think of little else in the weeks that followed. They were rehearsing for the re-run of *Grease*, but their minds were focused on the band. Then someone came up with the idea to combine the two. It was decided that the fledgling group would perform two songs in the interval of the show. They gave themselves the name Six As One and chose 'I'll Never Break Your Heart' and 'We've Got It Goin' On', two songs which had helped the Backstreet Boys make it big in Europe that year.

As the re-run of *Grease* approached, the guys had the songs and the simple choreography for their mini-gig rehearsed to perfection, while a teacher at Summerhill was ready to provide the backing music on a keyboard. The bonus interval entertainment was announced at the

Hawkswell before curtain up and the excitement spread round the auditorium. *Grease* worked its normal magic in the first half of the show, and the audience was primed and ready for the interval act. Backstage, all the T-Birds quickly slipped out of their bikers' jackets and reappeared on stage in black trousers and loose white shirts, each holding a microphone. It was chaotic, mad even, but great fun, and they sang the two songs brilliantly before dashing backstage to reappear as the T-Birds. The reaction from the audience was incredible each night and the interval act seemed to steal the show.

Buoyed by the positive reaction to Six As One and their sudden fame, however modest it may have been, the six boys continued developing the band and their repertoire. They added new songs and more intricate dance routines and performed some other shows in small venues around Sligo. Things happened quickly, but almost as soon as they had got going they had to stop because Shane, Michael and Derek were occupied with their Leaving Certificate exams – the Irish equivalent of GCSEs. Once the summer holidays were upon them, Six As One went to work with renewed dedication. They worked hard on a dozen or so cover versions and Shane and Mark penned their first original song, 'Together Girl Forever'. But one aspect of the group everyone agreed was not right was the name, so they decided to change it. After considering dozens of options, they chose what seemed a modern, catchy name – IOU. It would prove to be the first of several name changes before the boys were ready for the big time.

Throughout the summer of 1997, the local enthusiasm for IOU grew rapidly. They performed several gigs at the Sligo community centre and other small venues, slowly building up a loyal following. All the shows were a success and were watched mainly by a few hundred teenage girls. The boys got stick from some of the lads at school, but, hey, they were having fun and were famous within the few square miles of Sligo. The summer of performing culminated in their biggest show yet – at the Hawkswell Theatre. They had made their debut there with a ten-minute gig, but this time IOU was the headline act and instead of two cover versions they performed a full show of sixteen songs.

Kian recalls: 'That whole period was great fun. We were getting recognised and talked about in the town. If we were doing a gig, we made sure every shop had a poster and we put adverts in the local papers. We were the biggest band in Sligo. We were like mini pop stars, but if we went outside Sligo, no one would have had a clue who we were.'

Throughout this period, Mary McDonagh was closely involved with IOU, helping them put together the shows, and two local men were also involved behind the scenes as unofficial managers. Now that some measure of success had been achieved, everyone was starting to see serious potential in the group to expand their popularity outside the confines of Sligo. But expansion brought complications. The two would-be managers became ever keener to tie the guys to a contract to guarantee themselves a slice of the action if things took off. They presented IOU with a weighty contract for their signatures and the sight of the proposal instantly brought a division of opinion within the group. Sure, they were all desperate to secure some kind of professional backing that might help them become pop stars, but not everyone was certain the two Sligo men were the best guys for the job. For a start, the contract involved tying down IOU for years and included complicated restrictions. Kian was excited about having people dedicated to the group and was in favour of signing, but Shane was dead against it.

As far as he was concerned, the contract amounted to the biggest IOU note the band could possibly sign and one they would be paying off for the rest of their careers.

Considering that Shane and Kian were the engine powering the group ahead, it was clear that the contract negotiations were a major obstacle. Shane says: 'It was a terrible contract, full of options and it was for something like eight years, which was crazy as we were so young. I felt very uneasy about the whole thing, even though we were all desperate to have a manager and get some support.'

Talks about the contract went to and fro for several months while the boys continued to rehearse and perform small gigs. They also recorded their first single 'Together Girl Forever', which was released on CD by a small independent record company and sold well around Sligo. The success of the single, coupled with the fantastic reaction to the boys' Christmas show at the community centre, increased the pressure on them to sign the contract. The two men were certain they could make IOU a genuinely successful Irish pop group – but they wouldn't make any investment until the boys showed them some contractual commitment.

The boys watched the *Smash Hits* Poll Winners' Party that December and saw all the pop stars strutting their stuff at the London Arena. They saw Five go up and collect the Best New Tour Act Award and just seeing all this happen in front of their eyes made them want success even more. But it also brought home to them just how little their local success meant. Shane and Mark in particular remember sitting there hoping that it would be them on that stage in a few years time. But, deep down, it felt just like crazy dreaming. The stark reality was that they were famous in Sligo, had one single out in the town, knew most of their fans personally, and were faced with a management contract that could in all probability ruin their chances of fame. For those dreamers on Ireland's west coast, the starry world of *Smash Hits* may just as well have been Pluto.

As 1997 drew to a close, the boys knew they would probably have to sign the deal and just hope everything worked out, but little did they know that in the background Shane's mum Mae had other ideas. Mae had seen what her son and his friends had put into their band and knew they were good enough to deserve better. When she saw that contract, she was determined they wouldn't sign and decided that instead they should have the top Irish pop manager in the business. Mae Filan had always taught her son to strive for the best and now she was going to get his group the best. That meant getting Louis Walsh.

5   Enter Louis and Ronan

L ouis Walsh is the man who took five young Dublin lads and turned them into Boyzone, the most successful pop band in Ireland's history. Six years on, those boys from the Northside are wealthy stars and their continued success has turned Louis into something of a hero among Ireland's teenagers. As Kian puts it, 'Louis is a god in Ireland. He's the man who makes dreams come true.' The trouble with gods is that they're pretty hard to contact.

Louis' Dublin office is inundated with phone calls, photos and demo tapes from hundreds of hungry wannabes, all dreaming of being the next Ronan Keating. When Louis is out in Dublin, it is not uncommon for a tape to be thrust into his hands followed by a quick-fire plea from an ambitious teenager – 'Listen to this Louis ... we're a brilliant band ... we're the next big thing ...' or words to that effect. He has heard it all before, either from wide-eyed youngsters or jaded talent scouts in the record industry. There are thousands of people out there who think they are the next chart-topping pop act and that all they need is Louis on their side and the number one hits will follow. So even Shane was sceptical when his mum said she was going to get Louis to manage the band.

He remembers: 'When my mum first mentioned it, I thought, Of course we need Louis, it's obvious, but anyone who wants to be a pop star in Ireland needs him as well. I thought she didn't have a chance, and we never thought in a million years she could even get to Louis. Every day we would see something about him in the newspapers and I thought you had to be someone important in Dublin to know Louis. All us guys thought that. But my mum was really concerned about the contract we had been offered. She was saying, "Don't sign that, it's your life, let me try and get in touch with Louis. He's the man you need."'

Mae Filan had one minor edge over the rest of the hordes angling for Louis' ear – they were both originally from Kiltimagh, in County Mayo. They hadn't known one another back then, so it was an obtuse connection, but anything extra that could help get her through to the pop maestro was welcome.

Mae set about her task with vigour. She was urged on even more when Shane decided to quit the college course he had started in Limerick to give the band a full-time commitment. He had become weary of the six-hour round trip by coach to join the other guys in Sligo for rehearsals every weekend. He also felt that going to college straight from school had been a mistake, so he decided to give the group six months' solid effort and, if things didn't work out, he would restart his marketing course the following September. His best mate Paul Keavney helped him get a job in Sligo's big DIY store, Buckley's. It was a decent enough job, but Shane got through his days in the storeroom, or helping in the front office, by singing and dreaming of being a pop star.

Now that Shane had chucked in his education, the need to get Louis Walsh involved became ever more important. Mae wrote letters, sent the IOU CD, and left many messages on Louis' answer machine. There was no response for a while, but then in late February 1998 she finally got through. She told him all about the band, their sound, their potential, the managers who were circling. Something in her voice convinced Louis that it was at least worth speaking to the guys and taking a look at the band.

Shane was in Dublin for the weekend staying at his sister Mairead's flat with Kian when the magical phone call from his mum came through. It was Saturday 28 February and the beginning of a remarkable three weeks that would change their lives forever. Shane recalls:

'Mum called and said she had spoken to Louis Walsh and that he wanted to meet us, but I wouldn't believe her. We had spoken about Louis before, but I didn't know she had seriously been trying to get in touch with him. She'd kept it secret, so I wouldn't be disappointed if nothing had come of it. My mum had to ring me back three times because I wouldn't believe it.

'I rang Louis and he told me to meet him at the Pod nightclub. He said he would leave our names on the door. Kian was watching television when I told him we were going to meet Louis. He was flicking through the channels and he didn't pay me any attention. He laughed and said, "Oh yeah, and my mum's going to meet the Pope tomorrow."

'I stood in front of the TV and told him again and again until he believed me. Then I said, "Wear something cool, dress like a pop star – look like Boyzone!" This was the big chance we'd been waiting for. We got to the club at about 11.30. We told the guy on the door that we were there to see Louis Walsh and it was like, Oh yeah guys, course you are, and he tried to turn us away. Then Louis came forward and said, "Hi, I'm Louis," and we walked in right past that guy – it was so cool.

'I was so nervous, really scared, to meet Louis and I didn't know whether to shake his hand or bow. To people of my age who want to be stars, he's the man and just to meet him face to face was something for me and I was thinking, Oh my God, I'm talking to him. The first thing he told us was not to sign that contract, and then he said he couldn't manage us because he was too busy with Boyzone. But he said he would get us on TV and that he would let us support Boyzone on their autumn tour. We were blown away that he was even prepared to help us. I kept thinking, I've got to leave here tonight with something definite. All I got was that Louis would call me.'

Kian was also amazed by the night's events. He adds: 'At the end of the night we were buzzing. Louis said he would be in touch and said he would help us find a manager. We were jumping out of our skin. We didn't drink that night because it was too important to us, but we were on such a high. We were running down the streets screaming our heads off. We thought IOU was pretty big because of what we had done in Sligo, but now we started to think we were going to really make it because we had met Louis Walsh. In all honesty we had no idea just how much he could do for us.'

A few days later, Louis called Shane and gave him another example of what happens when he waves his magic wand – he invited him to Ronan Keating's 21st birthday party. The bash was on 3 March at the Red Box, a big bar and gig venue adjoining the Pod. Only Shane and Michael could make it to the party while the others stayed in Sligo. It was the night Shane had his first taste of the world of fame and it was an experience he will never forget.

He says: 'When Louis invited me to the party, I couldn't believe it. I went, Urrrgh, I'm going to Ronan Keating's birthday party! I was so happy it actually brought tears to my eyes. I was a Sligo boy going to a big showbiz party like that, it was amazing. At this stage, Louis was still saying he wouldn't manage IOU. He wasn't making any promises and was just giving us a night out, showing us what it could be like. I went out shopping and bought the trendiest clothes I could afford. I borrowed £300 off my mum, which was crazy money for me to spend. I bought a Calvin Klein jacket and thought, Great, everyone will notice this is Calvin Klein! As if anyone would care. I even bought a pair of sunglasses with clear lenses, like the ones Ronan used to wear. I thought I was the business and looked like a pop star, but I was so self-conscious about wearing the glasses that I took them off the moment I got to the party.

'The first time I saw Ronan there was a massive commotion. I heard this big roar and then he rode into the Red Box on a Harley Davidson motorbike with Yvonne on the back. The rest of Boyzone were in a car behind. It was amazing. Later, Ronan walked by me and Michael and we introduced ourselves. I think he knew we were coming, which was pretty cool. I said, "Well done to you, you're a star, fair plays to you," or something like that. I felt so honoured to meet him. I watched Ronan that night enjoying himself, moving around the room, meeting everyone. I saw what it was like being him, how he was so full of confidence. I so wanted to get to know him and be like him.

'There was one mad moment in the evening when I was standing in the toilet in a line of guys – and all the other guys were stars. There was Alan Shearer, the snooker player Ken Dougherty, Keith Duffy and Shane Lynch from Boyzone – and ME! I was standing there thinking, What the hell is going on here, am I dreaming? I couldn't believe all this was happening to me. I hated leaving Dublin after that party – I didn't want any of it to end.'

That particular party may have been over, but the real fun was just about to begin for all the guys in IOU. A week later, Louis sprinkled some more stardust over their lives when he rang and said quite calmly, 'I've got you the support slot at the Backstreet Boys concert.'

The American pop superstars were playing two gigs at the RDS Arena, one of Dublin's premier venues, and Louis knew the promoter was looking for a good support act. The Sligo boys were such big Backstreet Boys fans that they already had tickets for one of the shows, so to be told they would meet their heroes, then star on the same stage, was beyond belief.

Kian says: 'When Louis rang and told us the news, Shane and I were actually shaking. I'm telling you, we had tears rolling down our faces, we were hugging each other and jumping around. We were going to the concert as fans anyway, but suddenly we were going to be part of the show. It was like we were dreaming.

'Louis just told us to get three songs together, with the music on a DAT. He didn't give us any more detail than that. He just said, Do it, get it together. That's the way he works. He can tell how good you are by how you cope.'

It was an unreal situation. At one point, the six boys were in turmoil over an uninviting management contract which promised everything but guaranteed nothing. Then, a few weeks later, they were being guided by Ireland's pop guru and were suddenly supporting the biggest boy band in the world. Thank you, Mae Filan!

The amazing story of IOU's shot at stardom was the talk of Sligo. It made headlines in the local newspapers and a buzz went around the town and Summerhill College, where Kian and Mark were balancing pop stardom with preparations for their Leaving Certificates. All six boys found the enormity of the break hard to take in, but there was little time to soak up the glory because they only had a week to prepare their fifteen-minute set. They got together for hours each night after school to prepare the songs and rehearse some simple choreography. They went shopping at EJ's Menswear, a trendy clothes shop in Sligo where Kian had once worked on Saturdays, and bought some matching cream trousers and different coloured tops. In terms of pop music styling it was a modest effort and hardly touched the Gucci and Dolce & Gabbana garb which is favoured by Boyzone, but the IOU guys still looked sharp and stylish.

Their three-song stage act was equally slick and included 'Together Girl Forever', 'Everlasting Love' and, oddly, a cover of The Who's 'Pinball Wizard', which would be sung by Mark. The music was professionally recorded on a DAT and the guys were so paranoid about losing the treasured tape that they had copies made for every guy. That way, if anyone couldn't make it on the night, the show could still go on.

The night before the concert, all the guys were crammed into a small flat just a short walk from the RDS when they suddenly heard loud music from the arena. It was the unmistakable opening beat to the Backstreet Boys' monster hit, 'Everybody'. They sprinted to the venue, looked through the windows and saw their American idols sound-checking and going through final rehearsals for the show. Tomorrow, IOU would be on that stage.

As if supporting the Backstreet Boys was not enough, the date of the first show – Tuesday 17 March – was also St Patrick's Day. The whole of Ireland was in a party mood and the IOU boys could not have chosen a more perfect day to make such a stunning Dublin debut. The whole experience was dreamlike for the guys. They arrived at the arena to see thousands of excited fans milling around outside and then they saw the mass of seats slowly filling up. Backstage, the boys got to meet Howie, then Kevin and AJ, and then they played basketball with Nick and Brian. Was this all really happening to them?

As IOU changed into their outfits backstage, Louis appeared and presented them with a copy of the *Evening Herald* newspaper which boasted a picture of IOU and an article about their big break. Local radio stations were following up the story; it seemed everybody was talking about the boys and how they'd gone from performing at Sligo's community centre for a few hundred loyal locals to entertaining 8,000-plus screaming fans in the cauldron of the RDS.

Mark remembers: 'The whole Backstreet Boys thing was amazing. It was like Louis had waved his wand and it happened. We were so grateful to get a chance like that. For me, to meet anyone in the pop world was a privilege, but to talk to the Backstreet Boys was special for all of us. We are all big fans and they're like gods to us.

'We told them that we had started out by singing their songs and they were saying things like, "Hey, thank you, we're really honoured." I suppose I was a bit star-struck. I'd not met anyone famous before, but they were really nice guys, really down to earth, and they asked us questions about how we were getting on. They were really hoping everything worked out for us and we were able to ask them all the questions we wanted. We were asking about certain songs we liked and loads of general things.

'We were all a bit dazed. It was like, one minute the band was not really happening in Sligo, the next we were meeting Louis and supporting the Backstreet Boys.

'The two shows were amazing and the reaction we got from the girls was fantastic. They didn't have a clue who we were, but they knew we were Irish, so they loved us. The noise we got when we were on stage was like nothing any of us had experienced. The sheer size of the crowd was a shock.

'I just remember having a feeling of total happiness. I loved the whole thing – the atmosphere of being at the arena preparing for the show, everyone working to get it right, the rehearsals, seeing the Backstreet Boys prepare, watching their show. Everything gave me a buzz and singing on stage to that number of people was unbelievable.'

More excitement was to come very shortly. Watching closely from the wings at the Backstreet Boys concerts was Louis and he was impressed with IOU. He saw a group of raw performers who looked good, sang well and were admirably professional for such newcomers.

Sure, they needed plenty of styling, but he could tell they were hungry for success and their act, put together under pressure at very short notice, showed they had natural flair and were prepared to work hard. Above all, however, Louis had got to know the guys and he liked them and it was this that swayed his decision to manage them.

Louis says: 'When I saw them at the Backstreet Boys concert, that's when I decided to manage the group. Above all, I liked them as people. They are great guys who were desperate to be pop stars. I wasn't sure at this stage that I could even get them a record deal, but I wanted to have a go. I had always said I wouldn't do another boy band because I didn't think I could take a group as far as I had with Boyzone. I didn't think there could be another Boyzone. But it was the vocals that did it for me. I could see something special there, particularly with Shane and Mark's voices.'

When Louis told the guys he wanted to manage them, it was a sound that topped all those hysterical screams from the RDS. Suddenly, the dreams of becoming pop stars did not seem such a wild fantasy. With Louis on board, it now looked like a certainty. Sadly, with the good news, came some bad: he was adamant that the group would only work as a five piece. One of them had to go.

It was a shock that the group would have to be broken up, but the boys had long been aware that the template for all successful boy bands in recent decades had been with five members. Six was difficult to choreograph and looked clumsy on stage. As they returned to Sligo full of the highs of their success, it was marred with a hollow feeling that such a horrible decision needed to be made, and reached quickly so none of the impetus from the Backstreet Boys concerts was lost.

It was decided that Derek would have to go. Although he was a good singer, he was more mature-looking than the other guys, which everyone felt upset the cosmetic balance of the group. Within days of their return, everyone gathered for a meeting at Graham's house. Derek, it seemed, had got wind that something was up, but it didn't make things any easier. It fell to Shane, the unofficial leader of the group, to break the news, which made it particularly hard because the two were best friends at the time. Derek was devastated. A few days before, he had been on the way to riches and fame, meeting pop stars, performing in front of thousands, but now all those dreams had evaporated even more quickly than they had arrived.

It was a cruel decision for IOU to have to make, but what possible alternative did they have? Stick together, say 'no thanks' to Louis, try to make it on their own, go for that nightmare management contract that was still lying around unsigned? There was no alternative and they weren't the first group of friends faced with such a scenario. It is a common feature in the making of any group that changes are made until the magic recipe is found. It has happened since as far back as The Beatles and to any other group you care to think of – Boyzone, Backstreet Boys and Spice Girls, all have undergone emotionally charged restructuring in the search of the right balance. Sadly, Derek would not be the last casualty before IOU were ready.

During the weeks that followed, Shane, Kian, Mark, Michael and Graham worked hard preparing to meet various record companies. Louis paid for them to go to London for a weekend to record two original songs – 'Good Thing' and 'Everybody Knows' – on a demo tape, so he had something to play to the people in the industry. The boys also fine-tuned their harmonies on several *a cappella* cover versions. Around this time, Ronan came along to meet the guys, help Louis choose the songs and generally lend his expert mind to the group's development. As he became more involved, Ronan, too, was taken by the boys' freshness, their sound and their enthusiasm. It reminded him of the earliest days of Boyzone. He got on well with them and could see their potential and happily accepted Louis' offer to be their co-manager. It was yet another amazing blessing for IOU. They now had an incredible management line up that would guarantee maximum exposure, so, as they prepared for the first record company audition, everyone felt supremely confident that a record deal was a mere formality.

The first person they met was Simon Cowell, one of the most respected A&R men in the pop business. Among other discoveries, Simon had made a name for himself by turning actors Robson Green and Jerome Flynn into pop stars after seeing them sing during an episode of *Soldier Soldier*. More recently, Simon had helped create the boy band Five and had become known as the man with the eye, as well the ear, for a pop success.

Simon met Louis and the boys at the Westbury Hotel in Dublin and listened to them sing. He seemed happy enough and when he went off with Louis to discuss what he had seen, the boys sat around confidently predicting that he would offer them a record deal before the day was out. Everything else had come so easily to IOU since they had met Louis, so they felt certain that Simon was simply thrashing out the details of the plan that would make them stars.

They could not have been more wrong. Louis sat down with them later and delivered the hammer blow. Simon wasn't interested in signing the band. All he wanted was Kian, because he looked cute, and Mark for his great voice. Simon thought that maybe he could use them in some other group at some point. Unbelievably, Shane, who had been the leading talent of the group since the beginning, was not even in the reckoning, which was particularly hard for him to take in.

Kian remembers that day well. 'We couldn't believe it. The worst thing was that when Louis and Simon went off to talk, we sat around saying, "Oh they're probably discussing how much they're going to pay us." But Simon hadn't been impressed. We came in looking terrible that day. Our clothes were a mess and we looked like five guys from Sligo who didn't have a clue about fashion or anything. We let ourselves down and it was a shock. We were amazed that he didn't even want Shane and it was like, God let's get our act together here, what do we do, Louis?'

The solution was painfully simple: the group had to be broken down further and reformed. It had been hard enough dropping Derek, but now it seemed that everyone's place was in danger. The immediate casualty was Graham. He would turn 22 on 19 May and it had been apparent for a while that the age gap between him and the others was a problem. This had been highlighted after the audition for Simon Cowell, and so Graham performed two gigs in Sligo just after his birthday in the knowledge that these would be his last for IOU. He says: 'When I looked at the whole picture, I knew my age was a problem and I have a very strong accent which doesn't go down well in interviews. I was pretty upset because it was my dream to be a pop star, but I understood and took it on the chin. I put everything into those last shows because I wanted to go out with a big bang. The main thing was for the band to go to the top and I didn't want to get in the way.'

With the band now down to four, the initial desire was

to find a replacement locally to keep it a totally Sligo group, the place where the heart and soul of the group had been born. Unfortunately, it was soon clear they would have to make the search nationwide and the only way to do that was to hold open auditions at the Red Box in Dublin. It was here that two boys would shine brighter than all the others. They were Nicky Byrne and Bryan McFadden.

6 Nicky's Story

Name:	Nicholas Bernard James Adam Byrne
Date of birth:	9 October 1978
Place of birth:	Holles Street Hospital, Dublin
Star sign:	Libra
Height:	5ft 10in/175cm
Eye colour:	Blue
Parents:	Nicholas and Yvonne
Siblings:	Gillian and Adam
Schools:	Baldoyle Boys', St Nessain's Secondary, Plunket College

Family

I come from a very close family and I miss them all so much while I'm away. We're the type of people who come in from a day at work and sit around chatting about anything and are still there at two in the morning. I used to chat with my mam until all hours and I miss things like that. My mam has four sisters – Betty, Marie, Con and Bernadette – who are all married with kids, so there's a big extended family and Christmas is absolute chaos in our house. The presents fill an entire room and it's tradition that one of the grandchildren gives them out. It's great fun and we all love it.

My mam is Yvonne and she's the best mam in the world anyone could ask for – she did everything for us kids. She is very religious and goes to Mass every Sunday and I grew up going to Mass with her. I still have a very strong faith, but I can't go so often these days. I pray every night for God to look after my family and everyone I care about. My Nana is also very holy and she gave me a Miracle Prayer a while ago, which I know off by heart and say every night before I go to sleep. She also gave me a birthstone on a guardian angel to keep me safe while I'm travelling. It came from Africa and I keep it in my Filofax. I'm lucky to have a great Nana and Grandad. Sadly, my dad's parents passed away a couple of years ago.

My mam always told me when I was growing up that nobody is better than you, and you are no better than any other person. That philosophy has always stuck with me. I would never look down on anyone, but I would never look up to anyone either, no matter who I meet – we're all only people.

My dad, Nicholas, has also been a big influence on me. He has always been an absolute hero to me and my brother. He's also a really cool fella. He's a painter and decorator by trade, and he is also the singer in a cabaret band called Nikki and Studz which has been pretty successful. They were mad busy in the 1970s and 80s when they were the resident band at the Racecourse Inn in Baldoyle. The pub is just a few minutes from my house and it's where Shane, Keith and Ronan from Boyzone used to drink. I used to help my dad set up the gear when I was younger. He had a song book and I would sing with his microphone in the empty cabaret halls.

These days, dad's band only plays about twice a week at different places, but they still do lots of weddings and he is also a DJ at 21st birthday parties and karaoke nights. It was my dad's dream to make his living with music –

and maybe now he'll get some more bookings because of our band.

My sister Gillian is 22 and she works for Ryanair at Dublin airport. She is also a good singer and does a lot of karaoke. She was an Irish dancing champion right up from when she was ten. Adam is eleven and he's in primary school. He's loving every minute of me being in the band and collects all the magazines and newspaper clippings. He is so proud and wants to be in a band when he's older. He loves it when fans call at the house, especially at Christmas when he gets loads of presents. Adam has grown up so much while I've been away. I have a great bond with both Adam and Gillian. I love them to bits and would do anything for them. Adam has got a cool head on his shoulders and is really popular with younger girls and I know he is going to make my mam and dad really proud.

Growing up

I grew up in Baldoyle, which is a nice area in the north-east of Dublin. It's a very homely environment, with terraced houses, and it's the sort of place where everyone is good friends with their neighbours. It is growing up there that has made me the person I am today. We live only a ten-minute walk from the sea and it's only five minutes by car to the nearest beach.

I don't mind admitting it, but I was always quite a sensitive boy. If I came home from school and my mam was not in, I would cry at the door. Anyone who lived near me would tell you that. Even if she had just got delayed at the shops, I would think horrible things had happened. I'm a terrible worrier and I worry about everything. I take after my mam and even these days I worry all the time that everyone is OK. When I was six, I got the croup, which is a really terrible cough, and it was so bad I was put in an oxygen tent in hospital. It was only for a day, but it was the most frightening time for me because I hated being left on my own. I bawled my eyes out when my mam went home. But I had a great childhood and I couldn't have asked for any more. We weren't rich, but we never went without anything. We had some amazing holidays and one year we went to Canada. I really can't believe how lucky I have been in my life.

I used to hang around with about eight or nine lads and a bunch of girls while I was growing up in Baldoyle. We had some great times and there are a few connections in my childhood with Boyzone. Ronan grew up in Bayside which is just under the railway tunnel from where I live. I knew some of his schoolfriends and we had very similar childhoods and hung around the exact same places, but at different times. My house is only five minutes from where Shane and Keith grew up in Donaghmede, and my sister used to drink with them in the Racecourse Inn.

Football

I've played football ever since I was tiny. My dad used to be a good goalkeeper for a Dublin side and had trials for League of Ireland teams. He was known for being agile and very brave. He coached me and when I was five I played in mini-leagues and he used to stand behind the goal and would say, 'Go Nico!' when the time was right to dive at a player. I was brave like him and totally trusted his judgment, so I'd throw myself at anything and make the most amazing saves for a little fella. I nearly always played in goal, but sometimes at school or in games round the park I was an outfield player and I loved the glamour

Above Shane aged three

Left Budding young pop star Shane takes centre stage, aged four

Above A smart three- year-old Kian smiles for Easter

Right Kian celebrates his first Communion aged eight

Left Mark –
A bonny boy
aged one

Below Mark, aged
seven, and brother
Barry cuddle up
to Santa

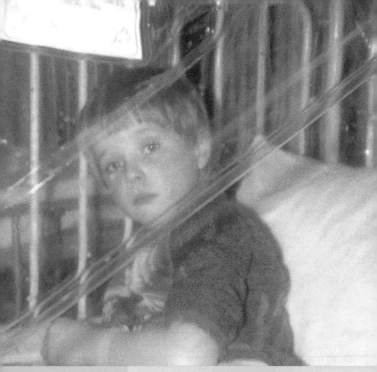

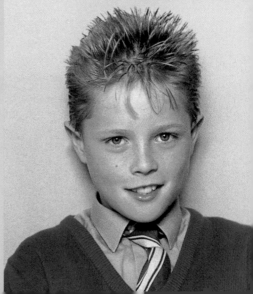

Above Nicky holds back the tears and the coughing in his oxygen tent

Right The first signs of Nicky's spiky hair, aged eleven

Above Baby Bryan begins to crawl

Left Budding young pop star Bryan, aged ten, plays on his synthesizer

Right Bryan is the leading joker in the group

Below The *craic* of being in Westlife. The guys laugh as they imitate the mad walk made famous by the Monkees

of scoring a goal. I'm a big Manchester United fan and my idol was Lee Sharpe. If ever I scored I would do those crazy dances he used to do at the corner flag.

I started playing in goal for Home Farm when I was seven and was there until I was fifteen. Home Farm is the top schoolboy club in Ireland and I got the best coaching possible. In the beginning, I played against boys who were three years older than me which toughened me up. We used to play against all the major schoolboy sides in Europe. One year we came fifth in Europe in an Under 12s tournament in Belgium and played against the likes of Barcelona and AC Milan. It was an amazing experience and I won the Best Goalkeeper of the Tournament award. I got a huge trophy presented to me in the stadium. There were TV cameras and the press snapping me – it was unbelievable and one of the proudest moments of my life.

I was looked over for the Irish schoolboy team for a while because the manager thought I was too small. A lot of people were saying that I was the best keeper around, but they always said, 'Nicky, he's a great *little* keeper.' That killed me and I got very angry. My height was a touchy subject when I was growing up and when I was fourteen I was so worried about it that I went to see a doctor. He had this chart where they work out how tall you'll be by taking your parents' height, your height and how many growing years you have left. I was 5ft 4in then and he said you'll grow to about 5ft 8in, which was a disaster for me if I wanted to be a goalkeeper.

The entire Home Farm back four was in the Irish U15 team – but I was left out because of my height. My manager asked the Irish manager to give me a chance and I made my debut for Ireland when I was fifteen against Switzerland in Zurich. We won four-nil and I had a good game, so I'd managed to prove them wrong. But the reputation of being a 'great *little* keeper' stuck with me and it wrecked my head.

Things started happening with big professional clubs when I was fifteen and I went for trials at Derby, Everton and Leeds United. I was 5ft 7in by this time, which was grand, but I broke my elbow while training with the Irish team. It was really bad and put me out for three months and I ended up missing the European Championship, which was a major blow. It would have been one of the highlights of my career. I had to have an operation and had two pins inserted in my arm, which are still there to this day.

After my elbow healed, I had offers to sign for Newcastle and Everton, but Leeds put an amazing deal on the table. The club even flew my parents over to England to see the set up and finally I decided to leave school and go to Leeds. I left in the fifth year without doing my Leaving Certificate, but promised my mam I would go back and pass it if things didn't work out. My mam was behind me 100 per cent, which is amazing when you think she was giving her sixteen-year-old son her blessing to leave school. Even though I didn't like going back to school when football was over for me, I kept my promise to my mam and dad.

School and Music

I went to Baldoyle Boys' National School from four to twelve and then to St Nessain's Secondary School. I had a great laugh at school. I was a messer, but I never really got into serious trouble because I got away with things that other kids got hammered for. The year head, Victor Kane, was also the football manager – which helped! I wasn't a bad student, but I certainly wasn't brilliant.

I was never top of the class and only got average grades. My worst subject was maths – I really struggled at that.

I was in the same class as my two best friends, Sean O'Grady and Colm Costello. I call them Skinner and Cos and the three of us were together all the way up from primary school. They are still my best mates and know me to the core. I never went on the hop [skipped school] or did anything really bad because I didn't want to let my parents down.

The first time I got up and sang in front of people was at my auntie Con and uncle Liam's wedding when I was six. I did 'Karma Chameleon' with my dad and I remember keeping my head down because I was so shy. I was wearing a brown velvet suit and had this bright head of blond hair. I did my first school play at about the same age and I remember standing at the front of the stage holding a globe and singing 'He's Got The Whole World In His Hands'. I didn't really get into plays and musicals like the other guys in the band. We did *Grease* at my secondary school and the teachers wanted me to be Danny, but I didn't have the guts to do it. I totally regret that now.

As a teenager, I was always singing, but I was too shy to get up on stage. My sister Gillian introduced me to a lot of pop music. I loved groups like A-ha, Bros and Take That. I was fourteen when Boyzone started and I remember watching them on *The Late Late Show* singing 'Working My Way Back To You'. I was with some friends and they were saying, 'God, the state of them, can you believe they're doing that,' but I thought they were brilliant. I was thinking, God, I wish that could be me, but I couldn't admit it. We videoed that show for Gillian and I watched it loads of times. From that moment on, I wanted to be in a boy band, but I kept it quiet from most people. A year or so later I was happy to admit I liked boy bands. I didn't care when the other guys gave me stick because I thought the music was brilliant. I played Boyzone so much when I was at Leeds that I got most of the others guys into their music, especially my room-mates Alan Maybury and Damian Lynch.

Georgina

I had my first kiss when I was about ten during a game of dares or something like that. When I was younger I went to discos and had slow dances with girls and would go out with them for a couple of weeks, but never much more than that. I'd never had a serious girlfriend until I met Georgina at school. As a lot of the fans know already, Georgina's dad is the Irish Prime Minister, Bertie Aherne, and we've been together for five years. The first time I saw her was when I walked into the classroom during the first year at secondary school. She was sitting at the first desk and I liked her immediately. She is very pretty and has beautiful eyes and there was something special about her from day one. I love a refined lady, a prim and proper person, and that is Georgina in a nutshell. I came home that day and said to my mum, 'I've found the girl for me.'

For ages I didn't know what to say to Georgina and she was so shy she wouldn't talk to me either. I didn't have a clue how to break the ice, so it was like, Today I will smile at her, and stupid things like that. I would do laps of the corridors in between classes, so I would pass her. I liked her for two years before I got to know her. Her dad was the Minister for Finance back then and she lived in an upmarket area of Dublin, and I thought that if I ever went out with her it would be like the love story in the film *Titanic*. I used to accuse other guys of fancying Georgina, but it was just my way of talking about her without letting out my secret. We were in two classes together and I looked forward to those lessons more than any others. By the third year, liking her so much was cracking me up and I had to do something. A guy in my class called Michael Heynes used to get the same bus home as her, so I got him to ask her if she would go out with me. He came in the next day and told me the answer was no. I tried to act like I wasn't bothered, but I was dying inside.

A year later, my mate Cos got Anita Tracey who was a friend of Georgina's to ask her for me. This time she said yes and it was the best news of my life. The first night we went out was the day before my sixteenth birthday. We went to a party, but we didn't start seeing each other properly until a few months later. I was really nervous when I met her dad for the first time, but he was great. We went out for dinner and it was nothing like *Titanic*. He's just a normal Dublin guy and he never hides that fact. He's not a snob or anything and goes down the local pub every Sunday with his family and chats to the other guys over a pint. Georgina's mam and her sister Cecelia are brilliant and I'm very close to them.

I think I loved Georgina the first time I saw her, but it was really strengthened while I was away at Leeds. She stuck by me through everything. When I came back I felt like a failure. I cried all the time and felt my life was going nowhere. Georgina always showed me the light at the end of the tunnel and she got me through my Leaving Certificate exams – all I did was turn up. I owe her an awful lot. We haven't got any long-term plans because we are both so young, but we are very happy. She's got a busy life as well and she doesn't mind the attention I get from the fans. If they come to the house, she talks to them, and when I'm in the UK they're always asking me how she is.

Leeds United

I had a big going-away party in the Racecourse Inn with some karaoke before I went to Leeds. It was very emotional for me and I sang 'Stay Another Day' by East 17. I also sang Boyzone's version of 'Father and Son', which was very special to me because of the words, 'I know I have to go away, I know I have to go ...' I also sang that at the audition for the band three years later, so that song means a lot to me. The actual night before my flight was the hardest and I cried my eyes out. The plane was at 8am and I was still awake crying at 5am with my dad sitting on the bed. I was excited about the opportunity I was getting, but I was going to miss my family, my girlfriend and my friends, and I was worried something bad would happen while I was away. I suppose I was also crying because it felt like I was leaving my childhood behind. I got very homesick at Leeds and the first time I rang my mam I cried. You can call me a mummy's boy if you like, but we're a close family and I'm a very homely person.

We were looked after brilliantly by Leeds and lived in a lovely big house for the first year. At the start of my first season, I was selected for the first team squad because of injuries to other players. I was only 16 and I was on the bench for the third Premiership game of the season, against Southampton. I didn't get to play but I thought it was the start of big things for me. It didn't work out the way I'd hoped. I was flying for the first few games, but my performance went down when one of the guys coaching the youth team started to affect my confidence. He has left Leeds now, but he was a hard man and the whole experience was awful. Other players couldn't perform because of him as well. In the summer after my first year, I trained really hard back in Ireland and I came back on fire to prove this guy wrong. I kept thirteen clean sheets in the first fifteen games and saved about four penalties. Then I didn't play well in one game and he dropped me. I hardly got any more games after that.

In the second year, we were living in a new training centre in the country and it was like a prison – it was actually facing a real prison. The rooms were like boxes and every day was the same – breakfast, training, lunch, rest in my room, training, dinner, back to my room. I felt like I was cracking up and I was really miserable. I was earning good money, but I wasn't happy. Near the end of my contract, the new manager George Graham told me they weren't keeping me on because I was only 5ft 10in. He only wanted big keepers, which seemed crazy because there were other keepers my height who were making it in the Premiership.

I was devastated and disillusioned with football. I went for trials at Cambridge and Scarborough and could probably have signed for a lower division club, but I no longer had the heart for football. I dreaded coming back to Dublin. I thought everyone would see me as a failure, but I had a chat with my mam and she said, 'Don't think like that. You got further than most kids ever do. Come back and hold your head up high.' My mam and dad were fantastic to me at the toughest time in my life.

Karaoke

While I was at Leeds, I had thought about coming home and starting up a boy band, but I knew you needed Louis Walsh behind it. Everyone was trying to get him, so I could see myself wasting two more years. It was hard being back in Dublin when some of my friends were now professional footballers. I worked in a clothes shop

**Nicky admires a Backstreet Boys quadruple
award. One day soon . . .**

called Alias Tom during the summer and was still
playing football for the League of Ireland, but it was
difficult to get enough time off to play. Working in the
shop was fine, but it wasn't for me and I felt like my
whole life was going wrong. I did my Leaving
Certificate in just one year at Plunket College and I also
bought a karaoke machine. I got all the CDs, had some
cards printed up, and from about November 1997 I
started doing karaoke nights in bars and at local parties.
I also did nights with my dad called 'Father and Son'.

Karaoke was great for me because I got the chance to fulfil my ambition to sing in public. I was really into Boyzone and did four or five of their songs each night. Everyone used to say I was good and that built up my confidence. I was desperate to be in a band, but I didn't know what to do. Loads of people said how much I looked like Ronan. Even when I was at Leeds, the guys nicknamed me Ronan because I looked like him and was singing Boyzone songs all the time.

Ronan was an idol to me and I saw him in a club one night a couple of years ago. He was with a group of people and I walked over and said, 'Ronan, can I shake your hand, it's an honour to meet you.' We shook hands and then I said, 'You're an absolute legend, fair plays to you, you're a credit to the country.' As I walked off, he came after to me and said, 'I appreciate you saying that, you're a nice guy, thanks for coming over.' I was smiling from ear to ear after that.

While I was doing the karaoke parties and my Leaving Certificate, I decided I would join the Gardai and become a policeman. It was something completely different from music and football, and I felt it was a good career, something I would enjoy. I thought police work would be challenging and fulfilling, but then my whole life changed again.

7 Bryan's Story

Name:	Bryan Nicholas McFadden
Date of birth:	12 April 1980
Place of birth:	Rotunda Hospital, Dublin
Star sign:	Aries
Height:	6ft/180cm
Eye colour:	Blue
Parents:	Brendan and Mairead
Siblings:	Susan
Schools:	Ardlea Road Infants,
	St David's Primary,
	St David's Secondary,
	Rosmini Secondary

Family

My mam's name is Mairead and she's a play school teacher. Our home is a four-bedroom house and there's a large garage which my mam had converted into a play school. She looks after about a dozen or so youngsters every day, which is pretty hard work. My dad is Brendan and he's an area sales manager for a pharmaceutical company in Dublin. I have one sister, Susan. She's three years younger than me and we're very close. Susan has been a successful actress for years and we spent a lot of time when we were younger doing shows and dance classes together. We were brought up in the Artane area on the Northside of Dublin, which was a good place to grow up. The only bad thing for me was that some local guys gave me a bit of hassle when I was younger.

Performing

I have always been a bit of a show-off and someone who likes attention. Ever since I was a kid I was always singing and playing up, acting the fool or whatever. I went to the Billie Barry stage school when I was about four, but I only stayed for a few weeks because I was too young to get into it properly. I re-joined with my sister when I was eight and that's when we started doing shows and really getting involved in the dancing. The first thing I won at Billie Barry's was a singing competition – the prize was a Cadbury's Easter egg.

I was nine when I did my first show. It was *The Wizard of Oz* and I was a flying monkey and my sister was a lullaby kid. I was in it for three months at the Olympia Theatre in Dublin – it was an amazing experience. I was only a little kid, but I was up on the big stage every night. It was so exciting; I couldn't believe my luck.

I stayed at Billie Barry's for about eight years because I loved it so much. I went twice a week – Monday nights and Saturday mornings – and made a lot of friends. I learned tap and jazz dancing and Susan and I did a lot of plays, pantomimes and musicals. I also did loads of auditions for TV adverts. Every year I was learning new things and doing different shows. Billie Barry's is a very good stage school, one of the best in Ireland. That's where Shane and Mikey from Boyzone went, but they were four years ahead of me. I remember seeing Mikey in a few shows, but I never got to know him.

Susan is a really good singer – better than me – and I'm sure she will have a career as a singer if she wants it. She was probably one of the biggest child stars in Ireland a few years ago and was the lead in shows like *Annie*, and she was in *Beauty and the Beast* with Lionel Blair. She was really famous in Ireland and I thought it was great at the time. People would say to me in the street, 'Are you Susan McFadden's brother?' It was cool. I never looked at her as being famous and thought it was really funny. It never bothered me and I was never jealous because I always had my own ideas of what I wanted to do – and that was pop music. Now Susan's getting all that fame thing about me, which is a turnaround. She was always in the papers in Ireland over the years and is probably glad it's me getting some of the attention for a change. She loves the fact that I'm in the group and always supports me in everything I do.

Ever since I can remember, I have loved singing. When I was a kid I used to sing in the shower, or pose in front of the mirror pretending I was Michael Jackson, Jason Donovan or whoever was in the charts. While I was at the drama school, I did about three or four shows at the Gaiety Theatre and I was on *The Late Late Show*'s Christmas Special performing with the Billie Barry kids. We did 'Greased Lightning' and other songs like that. I still have videos of everything I did on those shows. You should see what I look like!

I was also in a TV programme called *Finbarr's Class* for about three months, which is an Irish version of *Grange Hill*. I played a bully called Spot, which was odd because I was the one who normally got bullied at school. Sinead from B*witched was also in that show at the same time as me.

School

I first went to a pre-school in Ardlea Road, Artane, and I remember my first day there because I had something wrong with my leg and my mam had to carry me into the school and put me down in the chair. After that I went to St David's Primary, which was also in Artane. I was OK at school, but I was very lazy. My mam was the secretary at the school, so I had to keep my head down. She kept an eye on me big time and if I got in trouble I wouldn't be put up in front of the principal, the teachers would say, 'Right, Bryan, I'm sending you to your mam.' That was a much bigger threat and I would think, Oh no, not my mam!

My mam was tough on me because she would not tolerate messing in school and wanted me to get on with my studying. One time when I was ten, a student teacher was looking after my class and we were giving her hell, really causing trouble. We were so bad she couldn't take any more and had a panic attack and walked out of school in tears. There were five of us who had caused most of the trouble. The other four guys were sent to the principal and I was sent to my mother in the office. I used to collect stickers for the football World Cup in 1990 and my mam said, 'That's it, you're never getting any more again.' She stopped me collecting them and that was far worse than what happened to the other guys who just got a detention or something. My mam knew how to punish me, whereas the teachers didn't.

After that school, I went to St David's Secondary. I got on grand and didn't get into trouble or anything, but my mam wasn't happy with the school and took me out after the first year and that's when I went to Rosmini Secondary, which was great. I wasn't the best student, but I never got suspended in my life and all I got was a couple of detentions, mainly for lateness. I was good academically, but I was real lazy. One year we had an aptitude test and I had one of the highest in the school, but my problem was my work rate – it was way at the bottom. I would never bother studying for exams and would just get a C pass, never an A grade because I couldn't be bothered. In my Junior Certificate, I failed my mocks because I didn't do any work, but when it came to the real exams, I got my head down enough to get five honours and three passes. I could have been a really good student if I had wanted to, but music was always my life. I just wanted to sing and dance.

Growing up

I got a lot of flak when I was a kid because I was really fat, which was hard on me emotionally. It was not that I was huge, but I had a big belly and a fat face. I got called Fatso or Fatboy all the time, especially from some lads round where I lived, and it had a big effect on me. I didn't get on with those guys at all and I got all kinds of abuse from them. It hurt at first, but as I got older it just passed me by because I was so used to it. I got hassle at school as well, especially as I went to Billie Barry's and did dancing. Some guys thought you were a wimp for doing that after school. But all the stick I got went on for so long that the names just bounced off me. I accepted it and slagged them back and tried not to get too down about it. I got good at defending myself and was always the one who could come up with a smart comment, something really cutting. I'm still a wise guy now and come out with smart remarks, which can get me into trouble.

I was a lot happier in myself when I was at Billie Barry's. I felt I was part of something when I went there and I loved it because I felt like I was wanted. It was a very special place to me. Every Saturday night about twenty of us would go out and have a great time dancing. It was more of a social thing than a major dance place for me because I felt so at home there. But when I was about sixteen or seventeen I started taking it more seriously.

The two main teachers – Billie Barry herself and her daughter Lorraine – were very special to me. Lorraine did most of the teaching and she was great. She was kind and I sometimes spoke to her about my weight. Of all the people I look back on in my life and could say they were special, it is Billie and her daughter. They were two of the best and I wouldn't be here now if it wasn't for them. I don't know what I would be like, but I certainly wouldn't have got the confidence to stick with music. They gave me so much encouragement and they never put you down, so I have a lot to thank them for.

I also had a few really great mates, who have always stuck by me. Eddie Loughlin is my best friend and I've known him since I was three. There was always five of us in a tight group of lads – Eddie and myself and three other guys, Paul, Ian and John. We stayed together for years and never separated throughout school. Eddie in particular was always there for me when I was getting a hard time about my weight and he's still my best mate and I speak to him all the time. It has got harder to keep in touch with the other guys since we've all grown up and got busy.

As I got older, I was more conscious of my weight, so I got more dedicated to dancing at Billie Barry's and getting fit. I suppose the dancing was a bit of an escape. At one stage, I was doing hip-hop on Mondays, football training on Tuesdays and Wednesdays, hip-hop again on Thursdays, and on Fridays I'd go mad partying and dancing in clubs. On Saturdays I'd be back at Billie

Barry's dancing, and then Sundays I'd play in a football match. I was always doing something that helped with my weight. I also started going to the gym.

I did a few jobs when I was younger. I worked all summer when I was fifteen driving a forklift truck and got £5 an hour, which was great money. When I was seventeen I called out the numbers in a bingo hall. That was great fun and I really hammed it up and got £15 an hour for having a laugh. That was a mad job.

I served in McDonald's in the centre of Dublin for a few months and then I became a security guard there. I had to wear a uniform and it was the most stupid and dangerous job I've ever done. I had to stand at the door and stop the scumbags coming in late at night. I had no radio or backup and I was on my own most of the time. I used to catch junkies in the toilets and have to throw them out. There were always drunk blokes looking for a fight and something kicked off most nights. One night, some guy threw a Budweiser bottle at me and it smashed right against the wall beside my face. A big fight broke out and I said to the manager, 'That's it, I'm leaving,' and I resigned that night. He made me work two more nights because it was in my contract, but I didn't turn up for the last night – and never got paid either.

Girls

I've never really had a girlfriend that I've gone steady with for several months. I've maybe gone out with someone for a few days, on and off, but I've never got involved in anything serious. Girls were never interested in me because I was fat. It didn't depress me not having a girlfriend because I knew I didn't have a chance. But sometimes at school when other lads were talking about girlfriends and what they had done at the weekend, I would make up names of girls I was seeing. I had to come up with something because they would have laughed at me if they knew I'd not even got close to a girl. I was sixteen when I kissed a girl properly for the first time. She was at Billie Barry's and we went to the cinema in town with Eddie and one of her friends. We were supposed to be on a date and it was such a set up. I didn't make a pass at her in the cinema because I was really nervous. All the way through the film I was wondering whether to kiss her or not. Afterwards, we went for a walk and she took me off down an alleyway and snogged me. She was more experienced than me and I was afraid for my life. It was a great night though and after that I just went mad and was always kissing girls. I went from my first snog to having literally dozens within a few months – it was amazing.

I was in love with the same girl for eight years while I was growing up, but I can't give out her name. She was the love of my life and I thought about her every day – I still do, even now. She was at Billie Barry's and we used to sing duets together. Nothing ever happened between us because she was going out with another fella for five years and she loved him and she wasn't into me at all. I never told her how I felt during that time and it used to break my heart, just being with her. I wrote about five love songs about her and would have done anything in the world to be with her. Her personality is unbelievable and she has a great voice. I'm not the type who just goes for looks, I am into a girl's personality above everything else. She is getting into the pop business as well and I think she could do well.

Around Christmas time in 1997 we both went out and got drunk and I told her how I'd been mad about her all this time. She said she just wanted to stay friends because of this other guy, and that's hard to hear when you love someone so much. It was even harder because she was going through a bad patch with her boyfriend and I thought they might break up.

My confidence with girls went up when I went on holiday to Portugal in 1996. A few years before that I was too ashamed to even take my shirt off on the beach on holiday and I wouldn't even go in the pool because I hated my belly. By this time, the weight had come off quite a bit and I got a lot of attention from the girls. It certainly felt a lot better that way round, but I didn't get all big-headed or anything.

Since I've been in the band, I've been worried about getting involved with anyone. It's so weird because when I was younger I was so fat I never got any attention from girls, but now I get masses. I would love to have a relationship, and I'm disappointed I didn't get the chance to go out with someone properly before the band, because now I won't be totally sure if a girl likes me for my personality or for my image in the band.

Music

Because of my appearance, I never thought I could be a pop star. I always thought I stood a better chance of being a comedy actor, like John Candy. But when the weight started to come off, I realised I had a chance. I used to sing and play guitar in a band when I was about fourteen and I would skip classes to do rehearsals. We played some gigs at small function rooms and mainly did covers of Guns N'Roses and Cranberries songs. I had a really high-pitched singing voice, so I got to do all the songs that needed a female-type voice. When I was younger people used to say I had a great voice, but I never used to see it that way. I got into pop music when Boyzone came out, even though the other guys at school thought it was uncool. I got into it more and more and became really serious and I was well into the Backstreet Boys, Boyz II Men and Mariah Carey. Then I started a few boy bands, but I didn't get much further than sitting in the house with some friends, putting on tapes and working out some routines. We never even took it out of the house, but at least I tried to do something.

I left Billie Barry's when I was seventeen and by then I was into hip-hop dancing. I was also doing karaoke nights and was in a band, but that wasn't working out. I didn't know what I was going to do. Then, around December 1997, I was introduced to two guys – Tim and Darragh – and we started a band together. We called it Cartel and it was the best experience of my life – that is, until I got into this band. Me and the guys in Cartel just clicked straight away and we got a manager at our first showcase and started doing shows. We were together all through the first half of 1998 and everything looked like taking off – it was unbelievable. We were very tight, very together, and rehearsed every day for two hours after school in a big church. We performed loads of gigs around Dublin and got a following really quickly. We used to sing *a cappella* and were more into singing than dance moves. People loved it and we were becoming one of the most popular bands in Dublin. We would even upstage the bigger bands at gigs and had about 200 girls following us everywhere. We even got recognised in the street. I will never forget being in that band. It just grew really quickly and I'm sure we could have gone on to do something big, but we didn't have any money behind us, so there was a limit to how far we could go.

8 Perfect Harmonies

In June 1998, the Dublin newspapers and radio stations carried stories about auditions that were to be held at the Red Box. The first audition would be for a traditional Irish band – an all-male equivalent of The Corrs – which was being put together by record producer Ray Hedges, who had worked with Boyzone and was a good friend of Louis. The guys from IOU and Louis would look on at this audition to see if they could spot a young performer who could fill the vacant position in the band.

Nicky had missed all the advertising about the audition, but was told about it by one of his aunties. He listened to the radio on and off for two days, but never heard a mention of the audition. Finally, he called one of the commercial stations and a worker there tracked down the details for him. Nicky spoke to someone in Ray Hedges' office and was told to send in his details and a demo tape. Over the next few days, Nicky recorded three songs in the living room at home with the help of his karaoke machine. He chose 'Isn't It A Wonder', 'She Moves Through The Fair' and an old Irish song, 'The Town I Know So Well', then sent the tape off with his photograph. A short while later, he was thrilled to be invited to the audition, but to this day he isn't sure if anyone actually listened to his demo.

While Nicky had been busy with his formal application, Bryan was taking a different route to the audition. In fact, it was only by fluke that he went at all. Bryan was still working hard with Cartel and everything had been going well. In their short time together they had already built up a modest base of fans who followed the group to every gig, and some even waited outside the boys' houses. Bryan was happy in Cartel, but they had just been forced to sack their manager for not pulling his weight, so the group had a few problems. As with most other bands in Ireland, Cartel wanted Louis Walsh to take over the reins, so Bryan got hold of Louis' private number and called him. He finally got through and spent half an hour trying to convince Louis to manage them. Not surprisingly, Louis wasn't interested, but he told Bryan about the vacancy in IOU and said he was welcome to sing at the forthcoming audition. At first, Bryan felt it was disloyal to Cartel for him to go, but after days of agonising he realised it was too good an opportunity to miss.

Approximately 300 eager young singers searching for that elusive big break gathered at the Red Box for the audition. Each guy was given a number and waited at the balcony area to be called down to sing one song of their choice for a panel of judges sitting behind a table in front of the imposing stage.

Nicky had worn a black suit and looked cool, but he was a bag of nerves on the inside. He says: 'I remember seeing Bryan there. He had baggy trousers on and he looked like he should be in a boy band. But I also thought he looked a bit rough, so I didn't talk to him and just kept to myself and tried to focus my mind. I was number eighteen and when I walked up to sing I was psyching myself up and talking to God. Football had ended for me. I wanted this so much and I was saying, Come on, Nicky, give this everything you've got. It was an intimidating audition because it is such a big stage and all the other guys were watching from the balcony.

'I sang 'Father and Son', but I came in too early and I knew straight away I had it wrong. I thought it was a disaster and I felt sure I'd blown it. I had seen other blokes mess it up and say, Sorry, Louis, can we start again. I thought that looked unprofessional, so I kept singing. The girl who was looking after the music told the DJ to turn it off, which gave me more confidence because they obviously wanted to hear more. I ended up singing the rest of the song *a cappella*.

'I came down off the stage and Ray Hedges said, "That was good," and asked me to sing "She Moves Through The Fair". While I was singing that I could see Louis at the end of the table taking it all in, looking at me.

'About ten minutes after I'd finished, this guy came round calling out "number eighteen". They were on number 25 by now and I said I'd already been and then he whispered in my ear, "Louis Walsh wants to meet you." Everyone was looking at me and I was thinking, Oh my God, is this really happening? I met Louis and he said he was starting a pop group that was nothing to do with the trad band and he wanted me to meet the lads. At first I thought he said a *pub* band, so I was a bit confused.

'Louis came back a short while later with a guy from one of the newspapers and said, "I am setting up a new pop band called IOU, here's Nicky, take his picture because he's going to be in it." Then he walked off. My head was spinning. A photographer stood me up against the wall and started taking my picture, while a load of the other lads were looking at me.'

Nicky was introduced to Kian and later had lunch with him and Louis in the Chocolate Bar, a quieter drinking area which forms the third section of the Pod set up. They discussed the IOU situation and generally got to know more about Nicky. Louis was certainly impressed with his attitude and that he was keeping busy holding karaoke nights. He also loved Nicky's suit!

The rest of the guys were auditioned and twenty or so were selected for a second test to be held the following week at the Red Box. Bryan was among them and, by sheer coincidence, he got talking to Nicky towards the end of that first audition day. They immediately clicked and Bryan went along to the karaoke Nicky was holding that night on the other side of town. Bryan was convinced Nicky would get the one IOU place available, but they talked excitedly about the group and imagined how brilliant it would be if somehow both of them could be in the band. They sang a duet of 'A Picture Of You' towards the end of the evening, and anyone watching would have been excused for thinking that these two guys belonged in a group together.

At the second Red Box audition, Shane, Kian, Mark and Michael gathered with Louis to listen to the shortlist. Amazingly, Bryan nearly didn't bother going because he was convinced it was a foregone conclusion that Nicky had the job. When he finally decided to go, he didn't even make an effort with his appearance and just slung on an old shirt and some jeans.

The shortlist was quickly whittled down to six and then to just Nicky and Bryan, who had to fight it out while the others left the building. Suddenly, the huge stage at the Red Box seemed bigger and lonelier than ever as they took it in turns to sing again to a balcony of just a few people. Still, no one could separate them.

Next, they were asked to sing *a cappella*, but still there was no decision. It was like a boxing bout with the judges split on the verdict. Some thought Bryan was best, others wanted Nicky. So then they were asked to sing with the whole group to test the harmonies each boy added. It was an agonising, nerve-jangling time as IOU and Louis listened and discussed the strengths and weaknesses of the newcomers, trying desperately to home in on the best combination. Both brought a unique and perfect harmony to the group. Both added something and even Louis couldn't choose between them. Finally, it was decided that both guys would go and stay in Sligo to see how they fitted in with the band. If their voices were indistinguishable, then their personalities would have to be the deciding factor.

After a few days in Sligo, it was obvious that Nicky and Bryan got on well with everyone. They were lads who knew how to have a good laugh, but were also passionate about the group and were prepared to work hard. Their Dublin connection also gave the group an added dimension. After the stay in Sligo, all six guys returned to Dublin to perform a showcase at the Red Box for a record company. It was after this that probably the hardest decision in the short history of IOU was made. It had already been decided that IOU would be a five-piece and it was clear that the ideal choice was to take both new guys. A crisis meeting of the group was held at the Red Box and then Michael was given the shattering news that he was out. Understandably, he was devastated and everyone felt terrible for him. He had been in since the beginning, but had lost out at the final hurdle. He sat on a stool with his head in his hands for what seemed an age and everyone tried to comfort him, but he was inconsolable.

Kian says: 'Telling Michael he was out of the band was awful, the worst day ever. We were all in such a dilemma because we had grown up with him and he had been in the musicals with us and the band since day one. He's a great guy and he took it really badly at first. We would see him round Sligo afterwards and there was some bad feeling for a while, but then we saw him one night and he said,

"Fair plays to you all." I think he understands that we had to go with what was the best line up.'

It is ironic that all the guys had tickets for the *Grease* show starring Luke Goss at The Point on that fateful evening. They still all went to the show, but afterwards the new T-Birds that were IOU were Shane, Kian, Mark, Nicky and Bryan.

The first show to unveil the new-look IOU came in July as the boys headlined the annual Beat On The Streets roadshow around Ireland sponsored by 2FM Radio. The open-air concerts were staggered over eight weekends and it was amazing how the buzz about IOU grew. Thousands of teenagers attended the Beat shows and it was soon apparent that the boys were becoming a strong force in their own right with a hardcore of fans travelling to each venue from all corners of Ireland to see their new idols. Incredibly, during the week, Kian, Mark and Bryan were at school trying to get through their Leaving Certificate exams, while at the weekends they were being put to the test as pop stars.

For the Beat On The Streets gigs, the boys had rehearsed a short but tight show which balanced some *a cappella* ballads and a dance song, although Nicky admits he was the one who struggled most with the steps. He had been good at diving at a sprinting striker's studded feet, but spinning in time with four other guys was a whole different ball game. During this tour, the boys developed their own pre-concert ritual to focus their minds before taking the stage. They would form a circle together and pray moments before going out. As a final act of solidarity, they would put one hand each into the circle and lock them together, then count to three in Irish and shout the band's name: '*Haon, Dó, Trí* ... IOU!' It was a tradition they would always maintain.

A new addition was made to the boys' team around this

time and it was someone who would prove to be a crucial support to them in the coming months – their tour manager, Anto Byrne. Anto had known Louis for something like seventeen years and had worked for him with many different acts. He had also worked with big acts such as Van Morrison, Annie Lennox and Julian Lennon and had travelled the world with *The Commitments* star Andrew Strong. Louis had originally wanted Anto to be Boyzone's tour manager from their earliest days, but it had not been possible. Now that he had the new band, Louis called in Anto to look after them, but warned him that he was likely to need total commitment for at least six years. When Anto met the guys at the Pod they all got on well, so he took the job that would effectively make him the sixth member of the band. From then on, he would travel everywhere with them and make sure everything worked as smoothly as possible, from the moment the guys got up in the morning to the time they went to bed.

In between the Beat gigs, the boys showcased at the Red Box for all the major record companies. Now that the boys were a tight, well-balanced group, with big concerts under their belts, Louis really had something to sell and the A&R men were queuing up to have a look. The boys' confidence was sky high and this shone through during high pressure auditions in front of some of the toughest executives in the music business. Without exception, every record company offered the boys a deal. Fantastic figures and incredible plans were laid before them. The excitement grew by the day.

The final A&R man to see them was Simon Cowell, the man who had listened to them first as a raw Sligo six-piece. Shane in particular had something to prove here because Simon had originally not been impressed with his performance. But a lot had changed since that first audition in April and Simon could tell immediately.

He remembers: 'The difference from when I saw them at the Red Box compared to when I saw them at the hotel was like chalk and cheese. The chemistry just wasn't right before, but now I thought Louis had created something wonderful. There was no defined image or gimmick, they weren't trying to be all-out dancers, which was good, and I loved their sound and the way they looked.

'I have probably seen more than forty boy bands over the last three years and these guys just got me. Within thirty seconds I thought, I either play it cool and do the "Well, we'll come back to you" routine or I just tell them exactly how I felt. I'd never felt this way before and I just turned round to Louis and said, "I don't need to see or hear any more, these kids are amazing." He said, "But they've only just walked on stage," and I said, "I know, but they're unbelievable."

'Shane was a different person from the first time. He had really worked on his confidence and he really impressed me. I was impressed by them all. They did six songs for me and I asked them to sing a couple more because I was enjoying myself so much.

'Right then, I had this vision of these lovely looking boys who really have charm and voices of angels becoming a pop phenomenon. They were brilliant and really got me thinking. After the showcase, the boys were asking thousands of questions like lunatics. They said, "Can you make us into the biggest band in the world?" I said, "We'll give it a good go." Sometimes when you go to things like that you can wake up the next day with some reservations, but I thought this through and I couldn't get this band out of my mind.'

Kian remembers: 'After we sang all the songs, we sat down with Simon and he told us his ideas. All the other companies had done this and told us where they wanted

us to go, when a single would come out, the styling, that sort of stuff. Simon said, "I'm not going to rush you guys, I am going to get the right songs, the right producers, the right kind of styling, you're going to look amazing." We were listening and thinking, This is the guy for us. He knew exactly what he wanted to do and it sounded fantastic. He climbed all over the other record companies and is the best A&R man in the world. He was in a different class and we just clicked with him straight away. We totally trusted him and his judgment and he said to Louis that day, "Make sure you don't sign these guys to anyone else." We were so buzzed when we came out of that showcase, we were flying.'

Simon was not going to let IOU slip away, so as soon as he got back to London he fixed an urgent meeting with the lawyers at RCA and told them that this deal had to be closed fast, otherwise he was going to lose the hottest boy band around.

9 Westside Story

The record deal that Simon Cowell and RCA put together for IOU would turn out to be one of the most lucrative and positive that any new teen act could hope for. The finer details would take weeks to sort out, but it would provide the boys with a sizeable cheque of 'hello' money and a structure that could bring five albums and two greatest hits compilations. Most importantly, it guaranteed that the band would be RCA's new worldwide pop priority in 1999 and 2000. Even before anything was signed, the power of the RCA machine was felt immediately as the development of the band was put into overdrive. There would be no expense spared and the first of many top stylists were brought in to sculpture the group's image. Suddenly the outfits were indeed Gucci and D&G, not EJ's, and even the training shoes were the latest designer models at £200 a pair. Fantastic clothes were delivered to hotels in London by the suitcase-full. The whirlwind that would now guide the boys' lives for the foreseeable future had started to twirl the moment they secured their record deal, and the fashionable clothes were just tiny examples of the additions to their lives. Soon, a top choreographer was on board, followed by a fitness trainer, a press spokesman, hair stylists, photographers – even a biographer!

An ever-growing and changing cast would perform in the story of this pop group and play anything from the smallest walk-on part to an important cameo role. It was like the boys had passed the auditions and were now appearing in their very own musical, with the script changing and getting more exciting as each new page was written. Of course, they would always be the leading players, with Louis, Simon and Ronan holding the key production posts, no matter what changed in the wider cast list. They were the apex of a pyramid and everyone else filled the layers below. The boys all made one clear decision at this early stage – there would never be one dominant figure in the group. Everyone would be equal, no matter who sung what. Being at the top brings enormous pressure and although it was incredibly exciting now RCA were taking control, it was also quite scary. This pop music game was no longer a dream, it was deadly serious reality, and the boys had to deliver, or the pyramid would be nothing but dust in the desert.

From the moment he had seen them at the Red Box, Simon had been planning the songwriters he wanted to work with the boys. Among them were the respected songwriting duo Stevie Mac and Wayne Hector, who had two great new songs ready to go – 'Swear It Again' and 'Flying Without Wings' – which would be perfect for this new band. Simon had also flown the legendary pop producer Max Martin to London to watch video footage of the showcase in order to persuade him to work with the boys at Cheiron studios in Sweden. This was the studio where hits had been written and produced for the Backstreet Boys and Five, among many others.

For now, though, the emphasis was on one thing: supporting Boyzone on their UK tour beginning in September. And one of the first things Simon wanted for the group was a new name to go with their new styling and songs. No one really liked IOU. It added nothing to the boys' image and was hardly strong enough to carry the sort of international exposure they were due to get.

Dozens of names were discussed at various meetings as the boys rehearsed in Dublin for the tour. Finally it was decided the name would be Westside. It had a certain ring to it and seemed to emphasise the west coast roots of the band. Louis had come up with the name after seeing it on the side of a rubbish skip, of all things. Hopefully that wouldn't prove to be a bad omen for what was now the Westside story.

The opening night of the Boyzone tour would be in Bournemouth, from where it would move on to the major cities in the north before the key gigs in the 15,000-seater arenas of Manchester's Nynex and Wembley. The tour was a baptism of fire for Westside. They had played to many thousands in the open air Beat On The Streets concerts, but this experience would open their eyes and ears to what a truly dedicated fan following looked and sounded like in the intense atmosphere of an indoor venue. The boys had rehearsed their twenty-minute set of four songs *ad nauseam* and it was now perfect. It was certainly a mellow set for a boy band and included the songs 'Everybody Knows', 'If I Let You Go', 'Swear It Again' and 'Flying Without Wings'. But their show was an ideal introduction for the fans and would underline the vocal focus of Westside and dispense with any myths that they were yet another all-dancing five-piece with six-packs on display. The tour was a fantastic success and all the boys have mind-blowing memories of those heady first few weeks in the slipstream of pop stardom. Almost without exception, the Nynex and Wembley concerts have remained highlights in their careers to date.

Kian remembers: 'We didn't know what to expect on that tour. No one really knew us in the UK and everything had happened so quickly in the previous months. At the first gig in Bournemouth, we were sitting down on the stage with the lights out and we could sense the fans but not actually see too much. We were really buzzed. The fans could only see our silhouettes and when the lights went up, the noise just hit us – BANG! The screams were incredible, we couldn't believe the volume. We came off after our set and we were jumping around for about an hour, shouting, "Did you hear those screams?" The first night we played Wembley, we couldn't hear ourselves think. It was mad, crazy. You can't exactly describe what it's like walking out on to that stage. We never ever expected it to happen to us. It was just the most amazing dream. Wembley was definitely the highlight for me because it is such a big name, every band of any worth

Walking back after dinner at TGI Friday.

plays Wembley, and we were there just a few months after we got the final band together.'

Shane says: 'I had always wanted to play at Wembley. Simon Cowell was there, Louis, everyone from the record company, and our families. The place erupted when we came on. I was so proud to be on stage knowing that my mum was out there watching. She made the phone call that started all this off, so it was great for her to see what was happening.'

And Nicky remembers: 'The Nynex arena is massive and the seating goes up really high. The fans look like insects stuck to the wall at the back. There was like 15,000 people looking at the five of us on stage, it was incredible. I was thinking of all the years I had watched bands like A-ha, Bros and Take That and dreamed of doing this. Suddenly, I was getting a small taste of it. I was thinking, this is a dream, the best thing in the world – this can't be happening to me. It really was an unbelievable feeling. Just performing for those crowds was amazing.

'My mum and dad and sister came to the first night at the Nynex. Before we went out, the lights were on in the arena and I could see them and I was waving to them with a microphone in my hand. When we were on stage I couldn't see them because the spotlights were so bright, but when I went to that part of the stage, I waved in their direction. Every time I did that, about 6,000 fans went crazy. It was totally mad, what a feeling. Wembley was also special for me because of the name and its tradition with football. Every footballer wants to play there and suddenly I was playing the arena in a pop band. I was definitely happier to be there in the band and nothing to do with football. Even if I had the chance to sign for Manchester United tomorrow, I wouldn't dream of swapping this life for football.'

Bryan adds: 'The stage at Bournemouth was so

compact that when we were sitting waiting for the lights to come up, the buzz was incredible. Then the noise just hit you like a wall. I have never had such a high in my life. And then doing Wembley and Nynex – I couldn't believe any of it was happening to me.'

And Mark says: 'The noise at the big arenas just blew you away. I was like all the other guys, I couldn't believe this was happening to us so soon. It was amazing.'

It was clear from the reaction of Boyzone's fans that something special was happening with Westside. Yes, it was predictable that loyal Boyzone fans would be nothing but kind and welcoming to a new Irish boy band – especially as it was co-managed by none other than Ronan Keating. But it was more than that. The girls were reacting to the songs and the characters on stage in front of them. What Louis and Simon had seen, the fans were now seeing: five good-looking guys with charm and great voices. The hysterical reaction was repeated at every venue and if the cynics wanted tangible proof that the girls were genuinely interested in Westside, it arrived in the post. Thousands of cards introducing the names and details of the boys were printed and placed on every seat at each venue. The cards invited fans to send in their names and addresses, free of charge, to receive information about Westside. Within weeks, the RCA offices were deluged with replies and by the end of the tour the post bag had swelled to more than 10,000 replies. This unprecedented response came ahead of any wider marketing. The boys hadn't done any national press interviews, let alone appeared on television to promote a single.

The spontaneous buzz about the boys spread like a bush fire and soon the teen magazines were behind the boys and the national pop columns and TV shows began to take an interest. Even rival record companies started taking note of this hot new boy band. The music business regularly spends millions of pounds trying to create the kind of hype that happened naturally with Westside on that tour. But the best hype – the sort based on substance – cannot be bought, and this is what Westside were generating.

With all the attention, all the expectation, came the pressure. The boys had only been together for barely four months, and in that time their young heads had soaked up the kind of experiences that rarely happen in a lifetime of performing. They had gone from the Sligo community centre to performing on the biggest stages in the UK, on the same bill as one of the biggest pop bands of the decade. The record company responded to the excitement by piling on the commitments. Now Westside's diary was fully booked up a year in advance, with trips to far-off countries already in the schedule. Even the release date of the first single was delayed because the expectancy had risen to such a degree that it was felt a step back needed to be taken to make sure everything was perfectly prepared. The pace of the whirlwind had increased more than anyone had anticipated in such a short time.

The pressure on each boy was phenomenal and just adapting to this crazy new lifestyle was tough. As the newcomers, Nicky and Bryan were still trying their best to settle in and get to know the other guys. Shane and Mark, as the natural lead singers, were carrying the bulk of the performing pressure. And the communications man, Kian, was dealing with dozens of calls a day about every aspect of Westside on top of keeping his stage act together. It was inevitable that petty squabbles would occur in such a tight and pressurised environment, with so much at stake.

It had been very convenient for Westside to lap up the screams of the Boyzone fans, but if they wanted to succeed they needed to build their own following – and that meant grafting in smaller venues in less glamorous locations. So, following the highs of the Boyzone tour, the boys were brought down to reality with a big bump when they went straight back on the road touring Under 18s clubs and then with a BBC roadshow. This is the kind of gruelling slog every band has to do if they want their own fans. Boyzone had done this around Ireland in the early days and it had taken them six years to get to the stage of filling Wembley. Westside had walked out and enjoyed that buzz after five minutes in the business. Now they needed to hone their performance on a smaller scale and prepare themselves for the crucial *Smash Hits* Roadshow which was coming up in December. They would be competing for the Best New Tour Act Award and it was vital they had more touring experience. So, with their ears still ringing from the screams of Wembley, the boys squeezed into the claustrophobic space of their blue people carrier and hit the motorways. Their only luxury was a small TV and a video.

For the next few weeks in November, Westside performed at dozens of venues to crowds as small as 300, which was a shock after the buzz of performing for 15,000-plus. Tension built between the guys as one mini-gig blurred into the next, with one broken night's sleep followed by another boring motorway journey. The squabbling became more heated, more regular, the comments more cutting. There were even stand-up rows about who got the back seat for how long, who had it last and who would get it next. It got so petty they were even booking the most comfortable position a day in advance. The blue van became like a pressure cooker with five strong, tired personalities bubbling in a stew of emotions. All the time, their road manager Anto, the impartial mediator, was trying to maintain some order by stifling the rows to keep the show running. As the tour drew to a close, Westside were due to play the NEC in Birmingham, one of the more glamorous gigs, but by this time they were so fed up they could have been headlining Wembley Stadium and it wouldn't have made a difference.

It was Wednesday 25 November, in a car park as they left for the NEC, when the lid of the pressure cooker finally exploded. Anto stopped the van and cut through the bickering in the back with ice cold seriousness: 'Right. Shut up – all of you,' he said. 'Either I drive to the airport and we go back to Ireland and finish all this for good. Or I drive to the show. It's your choice. What's it to be?'

Silence. Then Kian, who was sitting in the front, leant over the seat and delivered a speech that marked a turning point for the group.

He recalls the scene: 'We were all tired and getting on each other's nerves. We had been thrown together 24 hours a day, seven days a week and were at breaking point. So much was going our way, yet we were arguing. It was madness.

'I shouted at them, "Just look at what we have. We've got Louis Walsh and Ronan Keating behind us. We've got an amazing record deal. Everything is in place. We have the *Smash Hits* tour ahead of us. If we win that, anything could happen for us. Everything we want could come true. But we're not going to get anywhere if we keep arguing like this. We have got to sort this out. Either we chuck it in now before we go any further, or we go for it. What do we want?"

'Everyone in the back shut up and listened. The whole atmosphere changed. Suddenly, everyone snapped out of it. We had always respected what we had, but we were losing sight of it and we needed to clear the air.

'A few minutes later, everyone was shaking hands and hugging and saying things like "I think you're great" and that kind of stuff. The atmosphere became positive again and that was a big moment for us all. After that, it was like, "Drive us to the gig, Anto. Come on guys, lets do it."'

Nicky adds: 'Kian was amazing that day. It was a brilliant moment, a real turning point. He snapped us all out of it, and as soon as we walked in the door at the NEC we had a positive attitude. There were loads of other bands there and they were really looking up to us and saying they had heard all about our record deal and what had been happening to us. We felt fantastic going on stage. Before that day, we had been thinking and feeling like five individuals who had been thrown together. But suddenly we felt like a band, five people working together for the same thing. It was a good feeling and we did a great gig. That argument had brought us together and made us stronger.'

On the way back from Birmingham, the guys put a video on in the people carrier and laughed all the way back to their hotel. Appropriately, the film they watched was *The Commitments*, the story of an Irish band that tastes success only to throw it all away in a mess of fall-outs and personality clashes. After the row and the triumph of Birmingham, Westside were fully committed to a different ending to their script.

This newly found unity within Westside gave the boys more confidence and energy for arguably their most important test up to that point – the *Smash Hits* Roadshow. The Roadshow, and the Poll Winners' Party that is its climax, is the key to breaking a new pop band. It is where New Kids On The Block, Take That, Boyzone and the Backstreet Boys all got their big breaks in the UK by being voted the Best New Tour Act. It was crucial Westside joined that roll of honour.

With that award in their sights, the boys huddled together to pray before each gig, then chanted '*Haon, Dó, Trí* ... Westside!' and went out to do what they do best – sing. They entertained the hordes of girls at each venue with soulful renditions of 'Swear It Again' and 'Flying Without Wings' and, as the tour progressed through Newcastle, Sheffield, Manchester and Birmingham, towards the finale in London, the following for Westside grew. There were more banners bearing their names among the audiences than for any other band, particularly their immediate rivals for the newcomers title, A1 and My Town. But, with the expectancy of victory, came the pressure to win the award. The tension was particularly heavy on Kian, who was taking calls from Louis and various different people at the record company, all eager to know how it was going. It was Kian's job to try to gauge the balance of votes the fans were putting into the bins for the three acts during the intervals.

Kian remembers: 'I was a ball of nerves every night. I was literally freaking out, losing it. Everyone was ringing me, asking how it went, how did the fans vote? Every night I snuck up to the back of the stage and watched the fans vote, and tried to work out which bin was getting the most. I knew we were getting louder screams than the others, but when Louis called me to ask for an update, I was afraid to say if we had won because I didn't want to get any hopes up.'

There was no real need to be fearful. When the tour was over, the boys headed back to Ireland for a well-earned break. As they collected their suitcases from the baggage carousel at Dublin airport, Kian's mobile phone rang for the umpteenth time. It was Michelle Hockley, who had been in charge of the *Smash Hits* Roadshow. Westside had won with flying colours. The boys all jumped on Kian and yelled with joy. As they walked through customs, a loyal contingent of Westside fans welcomed them home. Who better to have been there to share the wonderful news than the girls who were making it all happen?

Back in Ireland, life had already changed beyond recognition for all the boys. A small group of fans already knew their various addresses and would often call at their houses, or hang around for days on end outside. There were some snide comments from some lads – the jealous begrudgers – but all the boys could afford a smile when they saw the troublemakers from yesteryear who had given them a tough time. No one smiled more widely than Bryan, the boy they called 'Fatso' who was now getting the loudest screams at every concert.

Back in Sligo, Shane, Kian and Mark were pretty much local heroes. The two newspapers proudly documented their successes and everyone felt positive that they would crack the big time. The boys had already been paid handsomely from the advance for their record contract, but there were no real visible changes in the boys from Summerhill College. The one noticeable difference was the car Shane was driving. He loves cars and had always dreamed of owning a sports car. Back when he was working at Buckley's earlier in the year – when he had sung along to the radio in the back room – he had told his workmates, 'Don't worry, guys, I'll be a pop star one day and I'll drive round here in a lovely BMW.' That moment had arrived. Shane spent a large chunk of his advance on a BMW M Series with all the trimmings, and returned to Buckley's in a flash of silver. Shane says: 'They were all nice guys and had seen what was happening with the band. They were really good to me and said, "Fair plays to you." It felt good to go back in the car and show the lads that everything was working out just like I'd said it would.'

The boys returned to London for the Poll Winners' Party at the London Arena in December. It would be the most amazing party to cap the most extraordinary period of their young lives. They were only allotted the smaller dressing rooms, on the other side of the arena from the main stars, but Westside weren't bothered. They felt honoured to be there and would have changed in the street if that was required. A year earlier, the boys had watched this ceremony on television, their heads full of dreams. They had looked on in awe as the brightest pop acts collected their trophies and Five celebrated being the new stars on the block. Shane, Kian, Mark, Nicky and Bryan had all silently hoped that maybe one day, far off in the future, it would be them up on that stage clutching a golden disc, soaking up the adulation. Now, it had all come true in the most spectacular fashion in just twelve months. Boyzone's Steve Gately presented the Best New Tour Act Award that day, and as Westside came off beaming, Ronan and Louis were standing in the wings, cheering, smiling with pride. The boys gave Louis the trophy as a token of their gratitude to him for making it all happen, then they pleaded with *Smash Hits* to make five more copies. That was one award no one wanted to be without.

10 *Haon, Dó, Trí* . . . Westlife!

As 1999 began, Westside got their heads down and worked towards fulfilling the hype that was swirling around their every move. The amount of interest in the band from the media and fans was growing daily. The number of fans who had returned the Westside cards from the Boyzone tour had now reached 20,000 and high-profile shows such as *Live and Kicking* and *SMTV* were having the boys on to sing, ahead of any single. The reaction to Westside was in many ways unprecedented. They were generating a degree of interest in a new act that not even the Spice Girls had enjoyed. The Girl Power hype didn't really begin until after the release of 'Wannabe', which only went to number one in its second week after entering the charts at number three.

Clearly, Ronan's involvement had given the boys a massive headstart in raising their profile and winning media backing. But, more than this, Ronan's friendship and advice was proving invaluable as the pressure increased in the run-up to the single release. He had become a good friend to all of them and they'd spent fun times at Ronan and Yvonne's country home. A year earlier he had been their idol; now he was a pal and they were swimming in his indoor pool and having dinner in his mansion. Ronan was on hand to offer personal advice on all aspects of pop fame, including handling everyone from the media and fans to those who envied Westside's meteoric success.

Ronan was also there to advise them on money, from big matters like the complex record deal, to equally important things – like buying cars! Ronan proved his worth here for Nicky by securing a decent discount on a rare Peugeot cabriolet and promised to help Bryan when he was ready for something fast. Ronan's wisdom and general experience as a pop star were priceless. He had already lived and survived everything they were about to go through with dignity and grace and his sense of humour still intact. He was an ideal role model of how to cope with pop fame and not become a mess. As well as all that, he was proving an excellent guide to choosing the songs and planning recording strategy. Among the many pieces of advice he gave them, none were more valid than this: 'Be nice to people on the way up, because otherwise they won't be nice to you on the way down.' Westside were a long way from the downside, but it was a good reminder for them to keep their feet on the ground. However, if Ronan wasn't around, Louis was always there to give them a swift reality check if they ever became too full of themselves.

Ronan's support was never more needed than during the nerve-racking build up to the London showcase to be held exclusively for the music industry and UK media. Quite simply, this would be the night of reckoning for Westside. They had performed for thousands of enthusiastic fans, but it was a different game altogether singing for cynical music journalists, PRs and executives from rival record companies, people who had heard the hype and could think of few better ways to spend an evening than watching the 'next big thing' make an embarrassing hash of it all.

The showcase was scheduled for Wednesday 3 February at the Café de Paris, one of London's most exclusive nightspots. In the weeks running up to the big night, Westside rehearsed their set for hours every day until it was perfect. Ronan showed his support by constantly being on hand to calm their nerves and give them tips, whether it was how to hold their microphones or the best way to control their breathing while they were singing on a tummy full of butterflies. Soon, the boys were ready.

For Nicky, however, the week of the showcase would prove to be one of the most emotionally traumatic times of his life. The weekend before, his cousin Kenneth Sherlock was involved in a serious car accident on a main road outside Dublin while driving back from his girlfriend's house. Kenneth, who was only 21, was seriously injured when his prized canary-yellow Fiat Cinquecento collided on a bend with a police car. The exact details of the accident were unclear, but it happened in the early hours when the roads were icy and visibility was poor. Kenneth was left fighting for his life in a coma in intensive care for more than 24 hours. Tragically, he never regained consciousness and died in hospital.

Kenneth's family were devastated by his death, as were all his friends. Nicky was in London when he heard the terrible news. He had grown up with Kenneth and, although they were now living worlds apart, they would always have been as close as brothers.

The news shattered Nicky: 'I was in a terrible state. My immediate reaction was to get back to Dublin and be with my family and Kenneth's, but I was told I couldn't go home because there was too much to do for the showcase. I couldn't get hold of Louis, so I rang Ronan and explained the situation and he was amazing. I was almost in tears on the phone, my voice was quivering, and he said, "You need to spend time with your family. Right now, you need to forget about the record industry – I'll sort it out." He spoke to the record company and rang me back ten minutes later and said I could go straight home for the mass that was being held for Kenneth. I had about half an hour talking to Ronan and he was absolutely fantastic.

'Kenneth and I were very close when we were growing up. All he wanted in life was to be a fireman and for years he had been in the Civil Defence, which is a volunteer rescue organisation in Ireland. When people die, everyone always says they were so nice and all that, but it's true of Kenneth. He was a harmless, wonderful person. So many people at his funeral said how much they loved him. The police laid on an escort and the Civil Defence were there in uniform. Kenneth would have loved all that.

'I pray to him and I still cry about what happened. Kenneth was always a big support to me. He was like an agony aunt at times, listening, helping me. He was never envious, even when I bought a new car, or was in the papers for football, or the band. He was always so happy for me and proud. He even had a picture of the band by his bed. To think that his life was taken just like that, I can't understand it. It makes me ask, Why can that happen to him, and this can happen to me? Out of everyone, why did he have to be taken away? He was such a kind person. He didn't want a big life, he just wanted to be happy and be a fireman. What did he do to deserve to die so young? It cuts me in two when I think of his parents. They are lovely people who are suffering so badly and my heart goes out to them.' Sadly, Nicky had no choice but to miss Kenneth's funeral to be back in London for the showcase and for a photo session with Ronan for the cover of *Smash Hits*.

As the boys made their way through the West End of London, their nerves were jangling. There was the general hubbub of Piccadilly, with crowds milling around Planet Hollywood and the souvenir shops. By coincidence, a production of the musical *West Side Story* was attracting capacity crowds at the theatre directly opposite the Café de Paris, but it was across the road that you could sense a special buzz. A fortunate group of 200 or so of the most loyal fans had been invited to the showcase and they anxiously queued at the side door of the club. Around the front, a team of minders vetted the guest list and ushered the VIPs inside. More than 300 had been invited and they eagerly took up their positions around the upstairs balcony. The fans quickly filled the area downstairs up to the foot of a tiny stage, which had been built at what is normally the base of a sweeping staircase to the dancefloor.

The anticipation built. Ronan arrived, as did Keith Duffy and Louis Walsh. Downstairs, Simon Cowell, hobbling on crutches, made final checks to the sound system, while Anto buzzed around making sure the guys, who were preparing themselves in a backstage area behind thick curtains, had everything they needed.

The showcase was the acid test of the boys' nerve and talent, and from the moment they walked on stage and began singing they knew they had passed. They captured the attention of the discerning faces around the balcony and held it through a tight thirty-minute set of six songs. There were general nods of approval, and plenty of smiles as Kian introduced the boys with the cheeky twinkle never leaving his eyes. The fans surrounding the stage played their part by screaming at appropriate moments – especially when Bryan cued in for a solo section. When Westside confidently began 'Swear It Again' and 'Flying Without Wings', the girls were singing along word-perfect and anyone looking on from the gallery would have thought this young band were already veterans with several hit singles.

As the boys came off stage, Ronan was already there

to congratulate them. Kian remembers: 'There was so much pressure on us that night and Ronan had guided us through it all. This was a serious crowd, who weren't necessarily coming to support us. They were looking at our bad points, as much as our good ones, and when I came off stage I was like, Oh God, was that any good? I wasn't 100 per cent sure because it is so difficult to tell when you are up there, especially as most of the people upstairs were just watching, not cheering or anything.

'Ronan came straight up to me and gave me a hug. He squeezed me and all the guys and said, "Well done, lads, fair plays to you. You're really making it happen for yourselves." He was delighted and that made me feel a lot better because he should know if something like that is good.'

As the boys walked around the balcony after the showcase, the reaction they received was unequivocally positive. People waited their moment to step forward, shake their hands and wish them well. It was an incredible welcome from a hard-bitten cross-section of media types and it all bore testament to the natural charm the boys exude, as well as their professional singing display under intense pressure.

Out of all the well-wishers, there was just one man the boys wanted praise from that night – Louis. He has a simple routine of giving the boys marks out of ten as an instant guide to his opinion of their efforts. He is notoriously stingy with his scores and rarely have they got beyond seven or eight. Often, they have had to shamefully accept a derisory two, followed by clipped orders from their boss to shape up. A private drinks party for a select group was held at the Titanic restaurant after the showcase. It was there that the boys finally caught up with Louis. 'Well – out of ten?' they asked. 'I'll give you nine,' he replied matter-of-factly, but smiling. And that's all he had to say.

In the weeks after their triumph at the Café de Paris, the boys worked solidly every day in the UK doing interviews and photo shoots and appearing on TV shows. This work was interspersed with flying visits to various countries around Europe, where interest was already growing in the band. But the main emphasis during this time was on recording songs for the album and this meant flying to Stockholm to work at the 'hit factory', Cheiron Studios. Westside had already been here before Christmas and now there were more songs waiting for them to record.

Stockholm was under a fresh blanket of snow by the time the guys arrived in late February, so the city looked as beautiful as ever, but the temperature was well below zero and huge chunks of ice filled the waters that surround the islands of the centre. Freezing weather is hardly a distraction for five energetic Irish lads enjoying pop fame. They are so full of excitement about everything that is happening to them that they treat everywhere as if it were a beach in the Caribbean. Above all, it is their constant humour and sense of fun that keeps everyone smiling. Laughter is never far away when you're around the boys, although it is brought to an abrupt end when there is work to be done. For example, during a photo shoot for a German magazine in Stockholm, they concentrate and get the work done when the photos are being taken, but as soon as the clicking stops, the banter begins. All the guys get ribbed by the others at some stage, whether it's Mark for not wearing the right top, Nicky for his spiky hair, or Kian for having an unwelcome spot on his chin. It can be anyone's turn at any moment to get some stick. If one of them says something stupid, they are

The guys with their road manager Anto Byrne.

called 'Trigger' and suffer the added humiliation of having several hands mimicking the pulling of a pistol trigger at his head. This is a reference to Trigger, the name of Del Boy's thick pal in *Only Fools And Horses*. There is constant arguing among the boys about whether they are a Dublin or Sligo band, but with no real seriousness. There is, however, genuine determination in their frequent play fights which are conducted with gusto almost anywhere, even along the plush landings of Stockholm's Grand Hotel.

Working amid all the revelry is Anto, who is always there, taking a wise stance. He makes sure the guys don't step out of line, or take their high spirits too far, and he ends any disagreements that get too heated. He is the one who gets them to places on time, arranges the transport, the hotels, where to eat, and keeps track of the money. He controls the pocket money, too, which gets complicated when you're dealing with different currencies on sometimes a daily basis, and he is often seen using the calculator function of his mobile phone to work out the breakdown of a restaurant bill.

Anto is there for everything, from kicking the sleepy ones out of bed in the morning, to cooking meals at the studio, to keeping the boys going when they're feeling down and exhausted. He is on call 24-7, and, as his nickname 'Stats' testifies, Anto is also there to help educate the guys on all the new things they are seeing in this amazing new world.

Anto reveals: 'They call me Stats because whenever they ask a question, I usually have the right answer. If it's not right, I get a hard time. There is a real bond between me and the guys, but I like to keep a little bit of distance, so that I'm not their best mate. There has to be respect there, so when it comes to it, what I say goes. They respect my judgement and they know I will always be there for them. This is a 24-hour-a-day job and my phone is never off, but I am enjoying it. They are a great bunch of guys and I think it's going to get huge for them. They can see what is ahead of them because of supporting the Backstreet Boys and Boyzone and they all have the dream of being on that stage, not as the support band, but as themselves. These guys won't blow it because of any ego rubbish. We have regular reality chats to make sure everyone's feet are on the floor, and if anyone is obnoxious, they are told.

'The only teeth-grinding thing about them is the mornings. The worst to get out of bed are Mark, Shane and Kian. I can ring them and say, 'Get up, we're leaving in an hour' – and twenty minutes before we have to leave they will still be in bed. Sometimes I have to get pass keys and literally tip the mattress over until they are out of bed. They don't like me for an hour after that, but they come round eventually.'

At Cheiron Studios, any play-acting stops and the seriousness of what the boys are trying to do comes into sharp focus. The studios are a ten-minute taxi ride from the centre of Stockholm and lie in what can only be described as an incongruous location for what is the birthplace of so many pop hits. Cheiron, with its broken sign, is a nondescript one-storey building at the foot of a tower block of flats by a dual carriageway. From the outside it looks grey and lifeless, but inside the walls are filled with framed gold and platinum CDs from some of the world's top pop acts: Backstreet Boys, 'N Sync, Five, Ace of Base, all have recorded their biggest hits here. Upstairs are three separate offices, but it is in the basement that it all happens. A rickety wooden staircase leads downstairs to a corridor of heavy locked doors leading to sound-proofed studios. The only hangout area downstairs is a small kitchen where a portable television on the wall plays MTV and a few stools are scattered around a table. The walls downstairs are also covered with framed successes, and many more new ones, some still in their bubble wrap, lie on the floor, a space yet to be found for them.

Denniz PoP was the man who created most of those famous songs with his partners Max Martin and Herbie Crichlow. Tragically, Denniz, who was just 42, died from cancer two years ago. There are constant reminders of Denniz around the studios, not least the various trophies still on display in his old office and his name beneath most of the framed CDs. He may no longer be there, but the spirit of his pop music lives on with Max and the other talented writers at Cheiron. Most of the hit tracks from the Backstreet Boys' three albums and songs such as Britney Spears' worldwide smash '. . . Baby One More Time' were written and recorded here. This is the sort of company the boys are in when they work at Cheiron.

There was one serious problem that had to be solved while the boys were in Sweden – the band's name. There had been difficulties registering Westside in America for future merchandising and they were left with no alternative but to change it. This was a mini-disaster because the name Westside had already been cemented in the minds of thousands of fans and the media, but at least this problem had occurred ahead of the debut single. Besides, they had changed their name before and survived. New names had already been discussed with the boys at length, and one morning at Cheiron Kian took a call on his mobile from the record company to get confirmation of the final selection. He came off the phone and announced in the kitchen: "It's Westlife, guys. We're now Westlife." Everyone was happy enough and it seemed fitting that the name should be announced beneath the framed albums of so many stars.

With the new name confirmed and announced in the press, Westlife returned home to prepare for the release of 'Swear It Again'. It would be out first in Ireland on 29 March, then in the UK two weeks later. As if this pressure wasn't enough, Westlife also had to prepare for a big launch gig at The Red Box on 24 March for all the Irish press, to publicise the single's release. More worryingly, this meant that all the boys' families and close friends would be there to watch.

As the boys counted down the days to the launch, nerves were frayed to the limit once again. There was more pressure on Westlife than the average band releasing their debut because it had arrived after a full seven months of hype. The moment of truth was fast approaching and all the hype in the world couldn't save them if the single bombed. You can't make fans buy a song – they have to like it first.

Well, Shane, Kian, Mark, Nicky and Bryan needn't have worried. A crowd of 500 or more, including Louis and Ronan and all the key RCA executives, filled the Red Box and watched the boys turn in a near-immaculate performance. Yes, they appeared tense at first, but who could blame them when the eyes of all the people they care about were looking down at them from the balcony. Once the set was over, the boys breathed a huge sigh of relief in their small dressing room to the side of the stage and decided to go straight back out to sing for fun. This time the crowd loved them even more.

After the show, the boys were visibly relieved. Drinking in the Chocolate Bar, they hugged their brothers and sisters and chatted with their best friends. The feedback from everyone was 100 per cent positive – the boys had lived up to the hype. 'We're so relieved it's over and that it went so well,' said Shane. 'This was the hardest night so far for us, but it has turned out to be the best. I'm so happy – I feel like I'm floating on air.'

The celebrations continued into the small hours, but the boys were up early the next day for a live radio broadcast to begin promoting 'Swear It Again'. The next day, around 1,000 fans turned up for Westlife's signing session at the HMV store in Dublin and from there the guys began a promotional tour of Ireland, which included an emotional homecoming in Sligo.

All the work proved to be worthwhile a week later when the single went straight to number one in Ireland. But, as typifies the Westlife story so far, it was not just any old number one – it went to the top with record-breaking sales for a debut single and promptly stayed there for five weeks.

During the UK release week, 'Swear It Again' was neck and neck with Texas for a few days, but held on to easily take the number one spot on 25 April, which it held for a second week. At last the boys in Westlife could breathe a sign of relief; they had more than fulfilled expectations. They couldn't do any more than go straight to number one with their first single. Finally, they were on their way.

Kian says: 'It was fantastic to get number one and prove that we weren't just a load of publicity from Ronan's name. We have been so nervous in recent weeks because so much has been on our shoulders. If the song hadn't been a hit, we would have felt that we'd let everyone down. But you can't get any higher than number one, so we're well happy.'

Everyone was happy. The boys had slogged their hearts out to get that hit and they deserved it, as did the entire team behind them. Certainly Simon Cowell, the man who has been instrumental in turning Westlife's raw potential into polished chart-topping success, is proud of his boys. He says: 'In many repects they are my family. I've really taken them under my wing from the minute I first met them. They are prepared to work hard and they are really aware of how a team effort goes into a group like this.

'There are a lot of entrepreneurs out there who think boy bands are just a formula, but look how many fail. You have to respect the people who buy the records. They may be teenagers, but they're not stupid and I think they are the most discerning people in the world and they will never buy rubbish. Bands like Backstreet Boys and Spice Girls need to have three things – great voices, great songs and star quality. After that they need what I call the X-factor, which is something people either have or they haven't. I can't explain what it is, but I think Westlife has got it in abundance and that puts them on a different level to everyone else. I really do think they will become a phenomenon. This is just the start.'

There is no doubt that as Westlife embark on what will continue to be an extraordinary journey, they are rewarding the people who put such faith in them with tireless hard graft and by handling everything that comes their way with charm, good humour and an admirable degree of modesty.

Shane says: 'We appreciate everything we are getting. We will never forget the chances we have been given. We mustn't believe our own hype and must just keep working. I want us to be the best boy band ever and to be so successful that I can do whatever I want for my family. At the moment, Westlife have some fame, but it is only on a tiny level. I dream of us playing our own show at Wembley and maybe doing well in America and I want everyone to love our music. Who knows what the future holds for us.'

Kian says: 'I want to be able to go into a record store in a few years time and see three number one albums in the rack. I want that more than a fancy car and only when we have done that will I think we have made something of the band. At the moment it is Shane and Mark doing the leads, and Bryan is coming through, too. But the rest of us will sing as well when the time is right and the big objective is for us to be known as five great singers, where any one of us can take the lead. There is no lead person in Westlife – it is totally one band, no front man. Sometimes we wonder what we have done to deserve all this support, but that makes us more determined to work hard. Our lives are amazing at the moment and I wouldn't swap it for anything.'

Mark says: 'I can hardly believe everything that has happened to us. It was only a couple of years ago that I was watching TV dreaming about being in a band and making a single. It has all been amazing.'

Bryan says: 'If someone had told me a few years ago that this would be happening to me, I wouldn't have believed them. Just being in a group, singing on stage, being screamed at, is a dream. I sometimes worry what will happen when this is over, but I'm just enjoying it now. It's unbelievable.'

And Nicky summed up what has happened to them all quite perfectly when he added: 'It's like an angel has come out of the sky and asked us five guys, "What would you like to do with your lives?" The answer is Westlife.'

Epilogue

On 4 July 1999, the boys in Westlife made their way to Hyde Park to be part of one of the biggest music concerts in the world that year. The Party In The Park drew a crowd of more than 100,000 to the centre of London to watch an impressive list of top pop artists perform in aid of the Prince's Trust.

Prince Charles took his seat, along with an estimated global TV audience of 250 million, to watch acts including Boyzone, Pet Shop Boys, Geri Halliwell, The Corrs and Steps, to name but a few. And, of course, Westlife, who were there to perform two songs – 'Swear It Again' and their new single, 'If I Let You Go'.

The guys were celebrating the band's first birthday, and what a way to mark that anniversary. A year earlier, the final line-up that was to become Westlife had been decided in the Red Box. Now, after a whirlwind twelve months, those five guys were mingling backstage with some of the biggest names in music. They weren't hopeful hangers-on, or mere onlookers, they were part of the entertainment. This was their world now, a life that had once been only possible through the TV screen or pop magazines was now theirs to enjoy. They were inside the velvet rope of pop music. If they needed any further proof, backstage at the concert they were presented with their first gold disc – for 500,000 sales of 'Swear It Again' – and two days after the show they would fly to

Australia to begin a three-week tour of South East Asia. Was all this really happening to them?

It had been a remarkable journey from the Hawkswell Theatre to Hyde Park and, as the boys prepared for their slot, they could barely take in the sea of people waiting for them. The crowd disappeared into a blur across the park, but at the front were loyal Westlife fans, who had queued for hours to get a prime position, and they were waving banners. This is why Westlife were here and, as showtime approached, the nerves tightened and the adrenaline began to flow. Now was the time to focus. The banter came to a halt when the boys were called to the wings. Then, in the minutes before they were on, they huddled into a circle for their final ritual before singing. After their special prayer, Shane, Kian, Mark, Nicky and Bryan locked their hands in the middle of the circle, and only then were they ready: '*Haon, Dó, Trí . . .* Westlife!'

Acknowledgements

SHANE

First of all, I'd like to thank my mum and dad for all their love and support from day one. Without them I'd never have lived my dream. Thanks Mum – it all started with your phone call.

To Finbarr, Peter, Yvonne, Liam, Denise and Mairead. Thanks for guiding me and looking after me all my life. It's a long road ahead and I hope ye'll always be there for me, as I will be for you guys. To all my relations, a very big thank you.

Next I want to thank my management, Louis Walsh and Ronan Keating. What can I say? You've given me the chance of a lifetime. Thank you. To RCA, especially Simon Cowell, thanks for having faith in us – we won't let you down. Also, I can't forget to thank Boyzone for everything, Kenny Ho, Ben Mohappi, Paul Domain, Alan McEvoy, Richard Bray and our driver Marvin. A big thanks also to Rob McGibbon for the book – we love it and it's everything what we wanted to say.

To the boys – Kian, Mark, Nicky and Bryan. If I had to pick the band myself, I couldn't have picked four better guys. Cheer lads! (P.S. It's a Sligo band! Ha, ha!) And also to Anto. You've been there for us through thick and thin. You've done a great job, but you're also a great friend to us as well. Thank you, SIR!

To everyone at home in Sligo who supported us. It's

my favourite place in the world and we will definitely never forget ye. To all my friends over the past years, especially Paul, Keith, Graham – a big thanks lads. I'll see ye in The Belfry Saturday week!

Finally – to all our fans. I wouldn't be writing this without ye. As long as ye want us, we'll be here. (Oh, and to anyone I accidentally forgot, I'm sorry, but I'll catch you next time – I promise. It's only the start!) Signing off, Shane.

KIAN

I remember the first time I walked on to a stage, I was four and it was in the Silver Swan Hotel in Sligo. I knew after that I wanted to be on stage for the rest of my life. But it wasn't easy and I could never have done it without the help of my mum – she was always encouraging me in everything, from piano lessons, to tap dancing. My dad always helped me out with my music, he bought me my first guitar and anything I needed. And to all my family for putting up with the noise of different instruments coming from my room each night. All my friends for all the great nights out in Sligo, especially Paul Keivenigh and Graham Keighron – for helping me through my mad love life.

Now to the people that work behind the scenes. Our management – the mad but great Louis Walsh and our great buddy Ronan Keating (see ya in Benihana, Ro). You guys make it all happen; the prince of pop, Simon Cowell – you are a smash Simon; all at RCA and BMG worldwide – the work you guys have done for us, no words can say enough; Paul Domain for all the messing he puts up with; the guys who try and make us look good – our stylist Kenny Jo Jo Ho and our hair stylist Ben Mohappi, who always tries to keep it happy. I've got to

117

say thanks to Boyzone for all the touring we have done with them and for all they have taught us; the TV shows, magazines, journalists and photographers, and Marv – cos love don't feed him! A big thanks also to Rob for the book.

Last, but not least – the band. I love ya all and, of course, Anto – God love ya for putting up with us five. It isn't the easiest job in the world and without you we wouldn't be here today. Believe it or not, we love ya. Well, I think I have everybody and, if not, I'm really sorry, I'll get ya next time . . . Oh, the fans, as if I would forget ya! I love ya all for everything and we will always be here as long as you want us to be. Gotta go now and get some sleep – there's no rest for the wicked. Take Care – love Kian.

MARK

We have all had such an unbelievable year and what a way to be spending our first birthday. So many people have helped and supported this band and now I would like to try my best to thank them, so here goes . . . .

Firstly, I would like to thank the two people who brought me into this world, raised me, and made me the person I am today – my mum and dad. The two of you have always supported me in everything I've done, without you two, I'd be nothing. I love ye very much – thanks. To my two brothers, Barry and Colin. I've grown up with the two of you and had a great time doing it! I love the both of ye and thanks for the support.

To my best friend, Rowen – there isn't a funnier, sounder or more trustworthy person in the whole world – how lucky am I to have you as my best friend? You have been there for me through thick and thin and have supported me from day one. We always were and always will be a great team and remember – I'm always just a phone call away. Cheers, Bud! To my Nana Feehily and Granny and Grandad Verdon, all my aunts, uncles and cousins – thanks for all your undying support through the years. Also, my Gaga Feehily (RIP) – I love and miss you.

To our management – Louis and Ronan – thanks for supporting us and believing in us all the way and for getting us this far. (By the way – any chance of a day or two in Sligo?)

To everyone at RCA/BMG Records – thanks for believing in us. My thanks also to Rob for the book. To anyone involved in TV, radio, media and concerts who has helped us. Also my thanks to Paul Domaine, Kenny Ho, Ben Mohappi, Richard Bray, Alan McEvoy, Marvin and Trevor, and of course Boyzone – without all these great people we'd be in deep trouble! Cheers lads.

To all my friends and anyone I know back home who have supported us – thanks and I'll see you all in Equinox very soon. To all the fans – you are the reason we are here and we will be here for as long as you want us to be. Thanks for the support, keep it up.

To Shane, Nicky, Bryan and Kian – thanks for living this dream with me. It's a good craic, isn't it? You four have made it all possible and we'll have a ball. (P.S. It's a Sligo band!) To Anto – thanks for getting me up in the morning and sorting everything out for us – you're great to work with. Finally, to anyone I have forgotten to mention, I apologise and I thank you all. Mark XO

NICKY

This past year for me has been absolutely incredible. I'm living the best life anyone could ever live, but all this couldn't have been possible without the help and encouragement from a lot of people. Firstly, everyone at our record company, RCA/BMG, all the producers we've worked with, all the journalists, TV and radio stations that have featured us, thank you. I would also like to thank Paul Domain, Kenny Ho, Ben Mohappi, Alan McEvoy, John Reynolds, and all the Boyzone lads. Cheers to everyone from my home town, Baldoyle, you made me what I am today, thank you, and also to my teachers through the years.

My friends Cos (Colm Costello) and Skinner (Sean O'Grady). Remember, lads, Christmas Eve is our day! Also, to the rest of the boyz in Westlife – 'This isn't really happening to us, is it?' I love you all like brothers – long may it continue. I would also like to thank Rob McGibbon for a brilliant book – hopefully this is the first of many. And to Anto. I couldn't do your job without my hair turning grey – and by the looks of it, neither can you! Ha ha. I'm only joking. I love ya, Anto. Thanks for everything. Can I say a very special thank you to all the fans all over the world, you are amazing people. Our A&R man, Simon Cowell, you are one in a million. And, of course, our management, Louis and Ronan. Without you guys, this wouldn't have been possible. You are a pleasure to work with.

Most importantly, I'd like to thank my family. My mam, Yvonne, and dad, Nikki, my sister Gill and my little brother Adam. You mean the world to me, I can never repay you for the gift of life I have been given by you, and all the opportunities you gave me, but I'll sure as hell try! Georgina, what can I say? I love you, you stuck by me through thick and thin. I miss you while I'm away dearly. All my aunts, uncles, cousins, my new godchild Ryan, Nana, Grandad. I love you all.

One person I can never forget is my late cousin

Kenneth Sherlock. Ken, you're not with us anymore, but you'll never be forgotten, watch over us all and guide us. God – you're the man, thanks. I'm sorry if I have forgotten anyone, but there are hopefully plenty of albums and books to go yet! With love, Nicky.

BRYAN

I want to take this opportunity to thank all the people who made my life worth living and who got me where I am today. First, mam and dad, words can't express how much I love you. You have given me such a special life, you are two very special people. Sue, thanks for being a great sis, you are gonna be a star, I love ya. A special thanks to Ed for being my soulmate for the last fifteen years. You've always been there. To Nanny and Grandad, all my relations and friends, too many to name – thanks for all your support. Tim and Darragh – we had a great time and experience, best wishes in your careers.

I want to give a special thank you to Billie and Lorraine Barry, who trained me to what I am today. They gave me courage, strength and confidence – without them I'd be nothing. Gary Kavanagh, thanks for your help and encouragement; Louis, two words – THANK YOU – you turn dreams to reality; Simon – thanks for believing; Ronan – thanks for giving us your time, effort and advice; Boyzone, for giving us the break; our dream team – Kevin, Ben, Paul and Guy – thanks. To Steve, Wayne, Chris, Per, David, Max, Jurgen, Rami, Anders, Biff, Mark, Duck, Ro, Pete, Carl. And to Rob for the book.

Anto – I don't know how you do it – I love ya man. Nicky, Kian, Shane, Mark – love ya 4ever and last, but not least, thank you to the fans. You put us where we are today. Love Bryan.